D1008754

MAGNET SCIENCE

Written and illustrated by
Glen Vecchione

Sterling Publishing Co.,, Inc.   New York

For my grandmother and grandfather,
who made science come alive

Library of Congress Cataloging-in-Publication Data

Vecchione, Glen.
    Magnet science / Glen Vecchione.
        p.   cm.
    Includes index.
    Summary: Relates the discovery of magnetism, discusses the
principles behind it, and suggests experiments which offer a
"hands-on" explanation of how it works.
    ISBN 0-8069-0888-2
    1. Magnets — Juvenile literature.   2. Magnets — Experiments —
Juvenile literature.   [1. Magnets — Experiments.   2. Experiments.]
I. Title.
QC757.5.V43   1995
538'.4 — dc20
                                      95-20096
                                          CIP
                                          AC

10 9 8 7 6 5 4 3 2 1

Published by Sterling Publishing Company, Inc.
387 Park Avenue South, New York, N.Y. 10016
© 1995 by Glen Vecchione
Distributed in Canada by Sterling Publishing
% Canadian Manda Group, One Atlantic Avenue, Suite 105
Toronto, Ontario, Canada M6K 3E7
Distributed in Great Britain and Europe by Cassell PLC
Wellington House, 125 Strand, London WC2R 0BB, England
Distributed in Australia by Capricorn Link (Australia) Pty Ltd.
P.O. Box 6651, Baulkham Hills, Business Centre, NSW 2153, Australia
Manufactured in the United States of America
All rights reserved

Sterling ISBN 0-8069-0888-2

Contents

• • • • • • • •

1. Magnet Facts

Strange Stones

According to an ancient Greek legend, a young shepherd named Magnes discovered magnetism. It happened when the iron nails of his sandal stuck to a stone. He raced back to town and told all his friends. Soon, many people were curious about the strange stone and came to see it. Philosophers travelled far to study the stone, then went home to think about what it meant. In fact, many such stones were scattered all over the countryside and had been there for thousands of years. But the smart young shepherd was the first to notice something weird about them.

Perhaps, to honor Magnes for his great discovery, scientists gave the name *magnetite* to the strange stone. Magnetite has unusual magnetic properties. Pieces of it are called *lodestones*. The word lodestone means "leading stone," because a lodestone turns towards the Earth's magnetic poles like a compass needle. Also, when you bring certain metal objects near a lodestone, they stick to it.

From Magnes to Magnet

From Magnes, we also get the word magnet. You've seen magnets in different shapes and sizes, and you've used them every day. But magnets still puzzle most people.

Scientists describe a magnet as an object that attracts certain metals and produces a force, or *magnetic field*, around itself. This magnetic field comes together at the poles of the magnet, which can be either close together or far apart, depending on the design of the magnet. Every magnet has a north pole and south pole. Opposite poles attract, so one magnet's north pole will stick to another magnet's south pole. Poles that are the same push away from each other, or repel. A magnet's strength is strongest at the poles and weakest in the middle. It might seem a little complicated to describe a magnet this way, but magnets are certainly one of the strangest things in nature!

Only certain metals stick to magnets. These metals can also become magnets. Scientists give the name *ferromagnetic* to such metals. Ferrous means "containing iron" or "like iron." Things made of iron are most attracted to magnets, but things made of nickel and cobalt also stick to them.

When most people think about magnetism, they think about how ferromagnetic metals and magnets stick together. But did you know that magnets also attract metals such as copper, aluminum, and gold? Don't expect to feel any sticking, though, if you hold a piece of aluminum foil to a magnet — the attraction is so weak that only sensitive instruments can detect it!

Magnets, Magnets Everywhere

You may find it hard to believe that you use magnets everyday, but look around your house or classroom. How many magnets do you see? The door to your refrigerator might have some flat magnets holding up important papers. The inside of the refrigerator has a magnet to keep the door closed, but not locked. You might find a small magnet on the can opener. At school, your teacher might keep paper clips in a magnetic holder on the desk.

Some magnets are hidden in machines. Telephones use magnets. So do televisions, radios, and tape recorders. Anything with a motor, bell, or buzzer depends on magnets to do its job. In fact, you might say that wherever electricity goes, magnetism follows. When scientists realized this, they invented a new word: *electromagnetism*.

Finding What Attracts

What kind of everyday objects stick to magnets? Without thinking too long about it, how many can you name? You might feel certain that cans, nails, and paper clips do. Other things, such as keys, jewelry, and bottle tops, you're probably not sure about. It might also surprise you to learn that some rubbery things have magnetic qualities, like the soft magnetic pads on your refrigerator.

The question "What attracts?" has an easy answer: magnetic metals. But finding those metals in everyday materials requires some investigating. So, let's attempt to answer the question in a more scientific way by first collecting data.

FERROMAGNETIC SCAVENGER HUNT

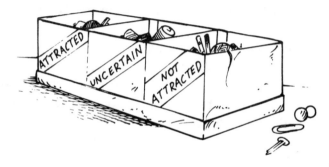

You Will Need

*Shoebox or small
   cardboard box
Shirt cardboard
Marking pen
Test objects such as:*

*Scissors
Ruler
Rubber cement*

*Paper clip, paper fastener, piece of chalk, eraser, marble,
rubber band, nail, safety pin, key, coin, small battery,
ballpoint pen, metal button, soup can, bottle top, toothpick*

1. Use the ruler to measure the width of your box. Do the same for the length of the box.

2. Divide the length of the box by three. Mark the top edge of the box to show three equal sections. If your box is 12 inches (30 cm) long, for example, you should make two marks, four inches (10 cm) apart.

3. Cut the shirt cardboard in half. Take the two pieces and trim them so that they're just a little wider than the box. Fold the edges and test to make sure that each piece fits snugly inside the box. Then glue the edges and place each piece inside the box at the mark along the top edge. You should wind up with three equal compartments in your box.

4. Use the marking pen to label each compartment along the side of the box. Label the first compartment "ATTRACTED," the last compartment "NOT ATTRACTED," and the compartment in between "UNCERTAIN."

5. Collect the objects on the list and any other objects that interest you. Look for objects — such as jewelry or fancy coat buttons — that combine two or three colors of metal. Place each object in one of the compartments, wherever you think it belongs.

When you think you've collected enough, place your box aside for the moment. In the next chapter, you'll test your objects and draw some surprising conclusions.

The Inside Story

What really happens inside a magnet and in the metals it attracts? A weird and wonderful dance of electrons! But before we talk about electrons, we need to look more closely at metals to understand how they fit into an even bigger picture.

The most complex materials in the universe are made from basic substances called elements. Pure metals — that is, metals that are not combined with other metals — are part of this group of elements. Billions of the same kind of atom make up a pure metal like iron.

Scientists know that atoms consist of a central mass of particles, called the nucleus, and individual electrons that move around it. The nucleus and electrons have opposite electrical charges. Different pure metals have different numbers of electrons moving around the atom's nucleus.

Electrons move in many different directions around the nucleus and form a kind of "cloud." In addition to this movement, each electron spins around its central axis like a little top. In some atoms, parts of the nucleus may spin as well. When parts of an atom, called *atomic particles*, spin, we say that they are *charges in motion* and have a *magnetic moment*. This does not mean that the atomic particles are magnets themselves, but only that their spinning motions can, under certain conditions, make the larger atom magnetic. Understanding these conditions will help explain why only certain atoms become magnetized and why only some substances are magnetic.

Spinning Close Up

Let's take a closer look at spinning electrons. While moving around the nucleus, electrons spin in either the same, or in the opposite, direction. Two electrons spinning in the same direction make the atom a stronger magnet; two electrons spinning in opposite directions cancel each other out. In

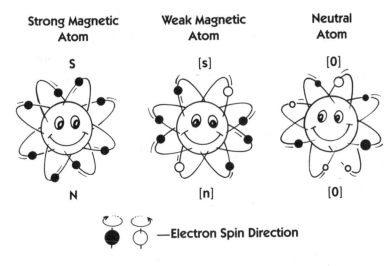

most atoms, the electrons surrounding the nucleus do not all spin in the same direction. This leads to a certain degree of cancelling out, which affects the overall magnetic strength — or *net magnetic moment* — of the atom. Substances made of atoms with strong net magnetic moments — that is, atoms where most of the electrons spin in the same direction — are magnetic. You already now about these substances: the ferromagnetic metals iron, nickel, and cobalt.

Less magnetic substances like aluminum or copper are made of atoms in which unequal numbers of electrons spin in opposite directions.

Finally, substances in which equal numbers of electrons spin in opposite directions are magnetically neutral. Scientists say that such substances, which include non-metals such as carbon, as well as the metals silver and bismuth, have a net magnetic moment of close to zero. But even these substances show a small amount of magnetic response when exposed to a strong outside magnet.

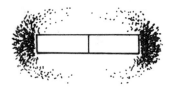

The Big Picture

Scientists classify substances into several groups according to the strength of their net magnetic moments. We know that the magnetic metals iron, nickel, and cobalt make up the *ferromagnetic* group. Scientists give the name *paramagnetic* to the metals aluminum, copper, gold, and several rare earth compounds. *Diamagnetic* substances such as silver and many non-metals are magnetically neutral. We'll look more closely at these classifications later.

Inside Iron

An iron nail can show us more about magnetism. We know that iron atoms have a strong net magnetic moment. So why isn't the iron nail a natural magnet? If each atom in the nail were a little magnet, shouldn't these little magnets eventually line up pole-to-pole and make the nail a magnet, too? With a little help, they do.

In the nail, billions of atom-size magnets do line up, but in random clusters called *domains*. All the magnetic atoms of one domain point in a different direction from all the magnetic atoms of a neighboring domain. To make a nail into a magnet, you have to dissolve the domains and force all the magnetic atoms of the nail to line up in the same direction.

CLOSE-UP OF DOMAINS

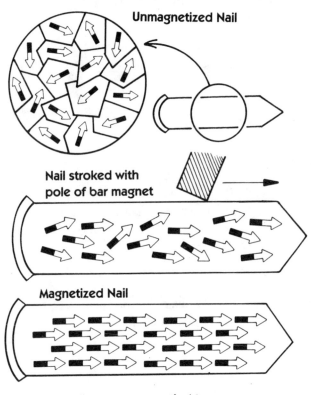

Unmagnetized Nail

Nail stroked with
pole of bar magnet

Magnetized Nail

S ⇨ — Magnetic Atom

The following project shows several ways to make strong magnets out of nails.

MAGNET MAKING

You Will Need
3 steel nails
Insulated copper wire
6-volt battery
Staples

Strong bar magnet
Hammer
Pliers

1. Use one end, or pole, of the bar magnet to stroke the nail at least 20 times in the same direction. Test the nail by holding one end against the staples. Stroke the nail a few more times if the staples don't stick to the end of the nail.

2. Magnetize the second nail by pounding it with a hammer. Hold the nail against the edge of a brick or other hard surface with the pliers, one end pointed north. Strike the nail several times with a hammer. This action shakes the atoms loose long enough for them to shift their positions towards one of the magnetic poles of the Earth. Test this magnet for attraction, too.

By stroking and pounding, you broke apart the many small domains of each nail. You forced the atoms to line up with each other, and the nails became magnets.

3. Wrap three feet (1 m) of insulated wire around the third nail. Connect the ends of the wire to the terminals of a 6-volt battery. The electrical current flows in one direction through the wire coils, creating a magnetic field that

comes together at the ends of the nail. Test this by moving the staples towards the nail. They should stick to the end. If you reverse the connections to the battery, the poles of the magnetic field will also reverse. When you disconnect one of the wires from the battery, the staples will drop from the nail.

Scientists call magnets made with the help of electricity *electromagnets*. Ordinarily, copper doesn't behave like a magnet. But copper wire becomes strongly magnetic when it conducts electrical current. Copper, and other metals that conduct electricity, help make powerful electromagnets. You've probably heard of these magnets. Suspended from a crane or derrick, they can lift huge amounts of scrap metal.

Electromagnets are very useful because you can switch them on and off. Imagine a giant electromagnet you *couldn't* switch off. Eventually, everything in the world made of iron, nickel, or cobalt would stick to it!

Permanent Magnets

Unlike an electromagnet, a magnet that you create by stroking or pounding does not lose its magnetism unless something happens to shake its atoms out of alignment again. Scientists call a magnet that does not depend on electricity a *permanent* magnet. But if you hold a permanent magnet over the flame of a candle, the atoms become excited and fall out of alignment. If you point your magnet away from magnetic north and pound it with the hammer, the atoms once again become jumbled and clump together in domains.

No one knows why, but pure iron makes a poor magnet. So scientists make the best magnets from iron combined with other metals. These combinations are called *alloys*. Steel, for instance, is an alloy of iron and carbon or iron and silicon.

Different Types of Magnetism

Although many types of pure metals exist, only a few of them show an obvious attraction to magnets. But many other metals, pure or not, respond to magnets, too. In fact, the atoms of any material, *metal or not*, always know when a magnet is close by. How do they know? By shifting around in mysterious ways. This shifting leads scientists to believe that different types of magnetic attraction exist, some quite difficult to detect.

Diamagnetism

The first, and most subtle, form of magnetic response fascinates scientists. They call it *diamagnetism*, and you can think of it as the natural magnetic quality of all matter. Even human tissue is diamagnetic. The atoms of a diamagnetic substance have a very weak net magnetic moment, and so the substance, magnetically speaking, is close to neutral. But even a neutral substance like human tissue responds to a strong magnetic field. For reasons scientists can't yet completely explain, the atoms turn slightly away from an outside magnet. This means that if you stand next to a strong magnet, the atoms in your body repel, rather than attract the magnet. This unusual effect has helped scientists look inside the human body by using magnetism. They call it *magnetic resonance imaging*. (More about this later.)

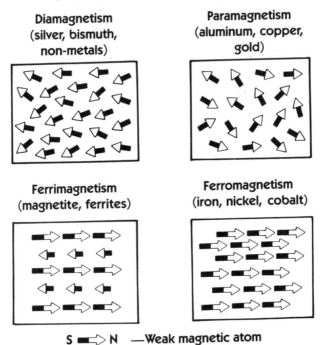

Diamagnetism
(silver, bismuth, non-metals)

Paramagnetism
(aluminum, copper, gold)

Ferrimagnetism
(magnetite, ferrites)

Ferromagnetism
(iron, nickel, cobalt)

S ⬛➡ N —Weak magnetic atom

Paramagnetism

Like iron and nickel, aluminum and copper consist of many magnetized atoms. But the atoms of aluminum and copper have weaker net magnetic moments—and so are weaker magnets—than those of iron or nickel. This means a weaker attraction to an outside magnet.

Scientists call the metals aluminum, copper, gold, and several rarer metals *paramagnetic*. You can detect their attraction to a magnet with a sensitive instrument called a *magnetometer*. As we'll soon see, slowing down the random jiggling motions of the atoms by cooling them causes some paramagnetic metals to behave more like ferromagnetic metals. This occurs because, in their naturally agitated state, the weak magnetic atoms have little chance to align or remain aligned for very long. To put it another way, if you make an aluminum pan cold enough, it will begin to behave more like iron in the presence of an outside magnet.

Ferrimagnetism

Let's go back to our lodestone for the third form of magnetism. Lodestones, made of magnetite, belong to a class of metals called ferrites. Scientists call these metals *ferrimagnetic*. The word looks similar to a word you saw earlier — ferromagnetic, as in iron, nickel, and cobalt. Ferrites do resemble ferrous metals in that they also show attraction to a magnet. But they will never stick to a magnet the way iron, nickel, and cobalt do. The reason has to do with the unusual behavior of atoms in the magnetite crystals. Most of the strong magnetic atoms in magnetite turn towards an outside magnet, but at the same time, the weaker magnetic atoms turn away. How can magnetic atoms of the same substance turn both towards and away from an outside magnet? The answer has to do with the peculiar crystalline structure of magnetite, which restricts the movements of atoms in specific ways.

Though magnetically weaker, ferrites are plentiful and soft enough to grind into fine powders. Combined with plastics, they make the flat magnets you stick to your refrigerator. Powdered ferrites also coat magnetic recording tape.

How Temperature Affects Magnetism

When you raise the temperature of a ferromagnetic metal beyond a certain point, its magnetism weakens and eventually vanishes. For example, when the temperature of iron reaches 800° C, it changes from ferromagnetic to paramagnetic. At 800° C and above, iron loses its magnetic qualities completely. The point at which a metal loses its magnetism is called the *Curie temperature*, after the French physicist Pierre Curie.

Different metals have different Curie temperatures. For instance, nickel loses its magnetism at 350° C. In each case, the atoms become too excited to remain aligned for very long.

Scientists have known for a long time about a class of substances they call the *rare earth metals*. At room temperature, most of these metals display paramagnetic qualities. But when you lower their temperature, they become ferromagnetic. By using liquid nitrogen, scientists have cooled rare earth metals to create new kinds of magnets.

Magnets in Action

Man-made magnets come in many shapes, sizes, and designs. At home, soft ferrite pads keep the doors of refrigerators, closets, and cabinets closed. Outside your home, slender rails lift high-speed trains off the ground. Both a car's speedometer and a vacuum cleaner rely on magnetism. Without magnets, tape recorders, VCRs, and computers wouldn't work — neither would credit cards or the automatic teller machines at banks.

You can find magnets everywhere, doing all sorts of jobs. Carpenters use magnetic nails that stick to their hammers. Astronomers use magnetic needles to find tiny meteorites. Chemists use magnets to filter metals from liquids. By using powerful electromagnets in an "atom smasher," we may soon learn more about the nature of matter.

To start your own magnet collection, begin by going outside and crawling along the ground. You can probably guess what we're looking for: lodestones.

ROCK HUNTING

You Will Need
Compass
Blue and pink chalk
Bag or knapsack

You will find lodestones wherever a good variety of rocks exists — near a quarry, a mine, or in any naturally rocky area. If you live near a desert, you can find many good lodestone specimens. Geologists often recognize lodestones by the way they look, but it's a good idea to bring along a compass and two pieces of colored chalk (blue and pink) to test and mark specimens.

Lodestones do not make very attractive garden ornaments. Most resemble grey lumps of coal, and some may have a grainy texture. They seem unusually heavy for their size. But the surest way to recognize a lodestone is to use your compass. Here's how:

1. When you think you've found a good stone, hold the compass away from it and allow the needle to settle into the north-south position.
2. Carefully move the compass against the stone. If either point of the needle moves towards the stone, a magnetic field exists.
3. Identify the poles of your lodestone by carefully rotating it against the side of the compass. If the north point of the

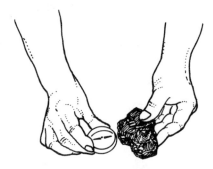

needle swings towards the stone, this indicates a south pole. If the south point of the needle swings towards the stone, this indicates a north pole.

4. Mark the north pole with pink chalk and the south pole with blue chalk.

As you continue to rotate the lodestone against the compass, you may discover that your stone has several north and south poles. These can be on the same side or on opposite sides. Continue marking poles with two colors of chalk. When you return home, replace the chalk marks with something more permanent, such as red and blue paint. Study the position of the poles. See if you can recognize the pairs. Label them A and B for the first pair, C and D for the second pair, and so on.

While you're at it, gather together the rest of your magnets and mark their poles with red and blue paint. Knowing a north pole from a south pole will come in handy for future experiments.

Man-Made Magnets

Because lodestones are ferrimagnetic, they aren't very strong. In fact, without a compass, it would be difficult to tell that they're magnetic at all. Exceptions certainly exist, though, such as the huge wall of magnetic stones that once pulled a West Virginia miner's helmet right off his head!

MORE ABOUT MAGNETITE

Lodestones have a very unusual history. In fact, the more scientists learn about the magnetite from which they're made, the stranger the story gets.

Magnetite is found in veins, or layers, throughout iron deposits. These veins can be very thick or very thin, but they are the only places that show magnetic activity within the deposit. Why should such an area of magnetism exist deep within a nonmagnetic iron deposit? Or, to put it another way, how does the magnetite get there in the first place?

For the answer, scientists looked at a strange bacteria that seemed to have quite an unusual life-style. It breathed without oxygen, enjoyed the dark, and loved to eat iron! When billions of these tiny organisms digested iron, they turned it into magnetic magnetite. As they died, they formed the magnetite layers.

Why should any creature, great or small, want to eat iron? Though it seems like a strange idea at first, iron is actually very important to some forms of life. Many animals have cells within their bodies that contain magnetite. Scientists now believe that such "magnetic cells" help certain animals find food or migrate. Honeybees, pigeons, tuna, dolphins, and whales all have cells containing magnetite in certain parts of their brains. Scientists now believe that the dolphin, for instance, uses the pull of the North Pole to tell up from down — important information for the dolphin when it must come to the surface to breathe. And whales often become stranded in areas where the magnetic field of the Earth shows some irregularity.

Even humans have small amounts of magnetite in their bodies. Though the amounts are extremely small and difficult to detect, magnetic cells exist in the lining of our noses. Some scientists now believe that at one time our noses were like compasses!

Scientists, especially physicists, and engineers, construct powerful permanent magnets. They combine ferromagnetic metals with each other or with paramagnetic metals to create special alloys. Some alloys become magnets very quickly, but lose their magnetism when their temperature changes.

Other alloys are more difficult to magnetize, but they keep their strength under stress. By combining metals, scientists can design the best magnet for a particular job. They can also design powerful electromagnets to carry out difficult and complicated tasks.

Think of places outside your home where you might find magnets. Look for inexpensive magnets in a science or stationery store. They come in many shapes and sizes.

Shapes, Sizes, and Surprises

As your collection grows, you can begin to separate magnets into groups based on size, shape, and function. The basic shapes include round magnets, ring magnets, bar magnets, U-shaped magnets, and horseshoe magnets. Then there are the soft, ferrite magnets made from powdered ferrite blended with plastic or ceramic.

For certain jobs, thinner magnets work better than thicker

bar or U-shaped magnets. Thin magnets work well against flat metal surfaces. Though weaker than thicker magnets, their larger surface areas make them especially useful for attaching paper to metal.

Round magnets have poles that come together on opposite flat surfaces. The round design shrinks the weaker, neutral sections of the magnet and allows for an even attraction throughout the body of the magnet.

You'll have a better idea of how well the design of U-shaped and horseshoe magnets works if you do the following test.

LIFTING A CHAIR

You Will Need
   Lightweight chair   *Tape measure*

1. Stretch your arms out from your sides and pretend that each hand is the pole of a bar magnet.
2. Try lifting a chair as high as you can with only one outstretched arm. Use the other arm for balance only. Notice how heavy the chair seems and how difficult it is to lift.

3. Have a friend measure the distance between the ground and the chair before you put the chair down.
4. Now stretch your arms out in front of you and pretend that each hand is the pole of a U-shaped or horseshoe magnet.
5. Use both arms to lift the chair. Notice how much lighter the chair seems and how high you can lift it.
6. Have a friend measure the distance between the ground and the chair.

Horseshoe and U-shaped magnets work well for lifting heavy objects because their poles, placed close together, combine strengths. Of the two, the U-shaped magnet is stronger because it's thicker.

2. Invisible Forces
• • • • • • • • • • • • • • • • •

So far we've looked at the shapes of magnets and at some of the jobs they do. We've also peeked at the mysterious, spinning electrons of their atoms. But what kinds of everyday materials stick to magnets?

A FLOW CHART FOR FERROMAGNETISM

You Will Need

Box of objects from your
  "Ferromagnetic
  Scavenger Hunt"

Poster board or paper
Marker or pencil
Bar or horseshoe magnet

What do the items in each of these boxes have in common?

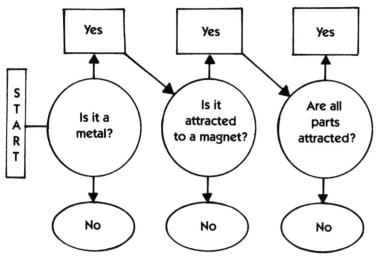

What do the items in each of these ovals have in common?

1. Copy the chart onto a large piece of poster board or paper.
2. Remove an object from your box and move it into the first

circle of the flow chart. If the object is metal, move it into the "Yes" box and continue to the second circle.

3. Hold the bar magnet against the object to test for attraction. Continue to the third circle if the object sticks to the magnet. You should wind up with three groups of metal objects: "ATTRACTED," "NOT ATTRACTED," and "PARTIALLY ATTRACTED."

4. Test all areas of the object for attraction. Count the number of objects in each group. Notice similarities and differences between objects of a group and between groups.

It might surprise you that soda cans, keys, coins, and jewelry won't stick to the magnet. But nails, washers, soup cans, and paper clips will. Just by looking at your objects, it's practically impossible to tell why some stick to a magnet and others do not.

Sometimes, a thin layer of one metal coats another metal. We call this "plating." Usually a more valuable metal plates a less valuable one, such as gold plating over silver, or silver plating over copper. But sometimes a paramagnetic metal such as brass plates a ferromagnetic metal such as iron or nickel. If you have a brass charm that sticks to the magnet, you can be sure that the brass is only "skin deep." Underneath lies iron, nickel, or an alloy of either.

How about partially attracted items like a ballpoint pen or a shiny yellow button with a dull metal back? The clip of the pen (made of steel, an iron alloy) sticks to the magnet, while the body of the pen (made from aluminum) doesn't. The back of the button (also made of steel) sticks, while the shiny yellow surface (made of brass) drops away. And just in case you haven't figured it out already — the "tin" of a soup can is actually a tin coating over steel, which attracts the magnet. The aluminum of the soda can, a paramagnetic metal, doesn't react to the magnet at all.

Seeing the Invisible

What does a magnetic field actually look like? You'll need some help to see one clearly. Even the Earth's gigantic magnetic field is only partially visible when radiation from the sun streams through the atmosphere. People living close to the poles can look up at the sky at night and see something fantastic. In the far north, scientists call it the *aurora borealis* or northern lights. In the far south, they call it the *aurora australis* or southern lights.

We can re-create a less spectacular version of the Earth's magnetic field and discover something about magnetic fields in general with the following project.

RE-CREATING EARTH'S MAGNETIC FIELD

You Will Need
  Bar magnet
  Iron filings (or a nail and file)
  Old pepper shaker
  Ruler
  Jar lid
  2 sheets of stiff, white paper
  Marking pen

1. You can make iron filings by holding an iron bar, a steel nail, or a similar piece of ferromagnetic metal with pliers and scraping it with a file. Collect enough filings to thinly coat a piece of paper.
2. Fold the paper and gently tap the filings into the old pepper shaker.
3. Measure the length of your bar magnet with the ruler. Find a jar lid with a diameter that matches the magnet's length.
4. Use the jar lid to trace a circle onto the second sheet of paper. Draw continents inside the circle, turning it into a

simple map of the Earth. Make sure you mark the North and South poles clearly.

5. Place the bar magnet on a flat surface and put the map over it so that the ends of the magnet lie under the poles. If the paper sags, fold the edges down to keep it level.
6. Carefully sprinkle iron filings over your map. Blow on the filings now and then to move them evenly across the paper.

Gradually, something amazing begins to appear: the magnetic field of the bar magnet, traced in filings, accurately recreating the magnetic field of the Earth!

Magnetic Field Facts

Forget the map for a minute and think about the bar magnet underneath. Notice how the magnet's lines of force come together at the ends, or poles. Study these lines. Can you find the strongest parts of the magnet? How about the weakest parts?

Magnetic fields look pretty similar for all shapes of magnets. Studying them helps you find the strongest and weakest parts of a magnet.

MAGNETIC PICTURES

You Will Need

*Assorted shapes of
   magnets,
   including a bar
   magnet, a
   U-shaped magnet, and
   a round magnet*

*Iron filings
Sheet of stiff, white paper
Pepper shaker*

1. Pour the iron filings in the pepper shaker.
2. Place the bar magnet under the paper and sprinkle the paper with filings. Do the same with the U-shaped and the round magnet. Try a ring magnet and some ferrite pads, if you have them.

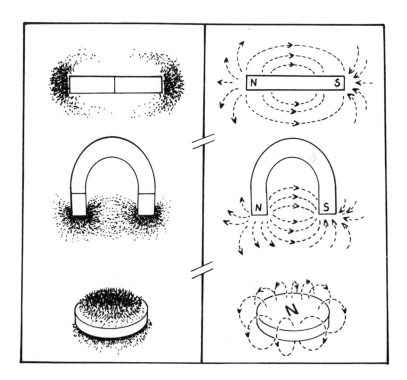

Notice that the magnetic field of each magnet has a different shape. With the round magnet, you may have some difficulty recognizing the poles. Round magnets have poles that lie on opposite flat sides of the magnet and not along the edges. If your round magnet is very strong, turn it on its edge and hold the paper over it. As you sprinkle the filings, you may see a magnetic field pattern that resembles the one produced by a bar magnet.

The shape of magnetic fields points out one of the most puzzling differences between magnetism and electricity: *dipolarity*. This term means that magnetic fields, unlike electrical current, always have two poles that can never exist apart!

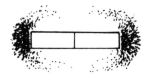

More and More and More of the Same

In the story of "The Sorcerer's Apprentice," the apprentice uses a magic spell to make a broom come to life and carry water. But even when he has enough water, the apprentice can't undo his spell. To stop the broom, he takes an axe and cuts it in half, only to see two brooms spring to life from the pieces. He cuts again, and four brooms appear. Soon the castle is overrun with brooms, until the sorcerer returns and saves the day.

If you break a magnet into two pieces, a north and south pole appear at opposite ends of each of the pieces. If you divide the pieces again, two new sets of poles appear. Try as you might, you can never get just one pole. In other words, breaking a magnet in half creates two magnets, not two pieces of one magnet. If you could break a magnet down to its atoms, what do you think you would find?

Let's try this out for ourselves.

THE SORCERER'S APPRENTICE TEST

You Will Need
Bar magnet   *Wire cutters*
Large, steel paper clip *Compass*

1. Straighten the paper clip and hold one end of it. Use the north pole of the bar magnet to stroke the clip 50 times, from middle to end.

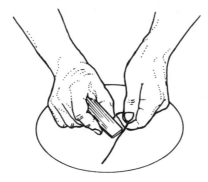

2. Hold the other end of the clip and repeat the procedure, this time with the south pole of the bar magnet.
3. Hold the compass near each end of the clip to test whether your magnetized clip has a north and south pole. If the compass needle doesn't swing towards or away from each end, continue stroking.
4. Have an adult help you with the wire clippers if you've never used them before. Cut the clip in half at the middle.

Immediately hold the compass against each end of the two new pieces. You'll find that each new piece is a magnet with a north and south pole like the original.
5. Cut these two pieces in half, and you'll have four magnets. Cut these four in half, and you'll wind up with eight magnets.

As the pieces grow smaller, the poles become too weak to show on your compass. But theoretically, you could continue making magnets all the way down to the individual atoms!

Magnetism Versus Electricity

Why is it that scientists can separate positive and negative charges of electricity, but not the north and south poles of a magnet? And how is it that electricity can travel in one direction without ever coming back, while a magnetic field always wraps around itself? No one knows for sure. Even in a complex machine like an electric motor, the magnetic fields collide and twist, but they never break apart or combine. This is because each field stays connected to its own poles.

Using iron filings, you can see for yourself how the magnetic fields of two magnets affect each other.

PUSH AND PULL

You Will Need
   2 bar magnets   *Sheet of stiff, white paper*
   Iron filings

1. Place the paper on a flat surface to catch filings that may fall from the bar magnets.
2. Dip the first magnet's north pole in the filings.
3. Dip the second magnet's south pole in the filings.

4. Over the paper, hold the first magnet's north pole against the second magnet's south pole.

5. Slowly pull the magnets a short distance apart. Since the north and south poles of the two magnets strongly attract, the magnetic field is strong between them at this point, and the filings hang in the air!

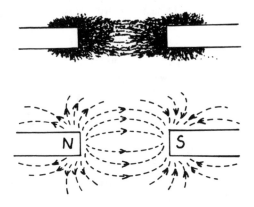

6. Dip both north poles in the filings.

7. Place the north pole of the first magnet against the north pole of the second magnet. You won't get far. Like poles repel each other, and the filings will show this repulsion by bending away weirdly from the ends of the magnets.

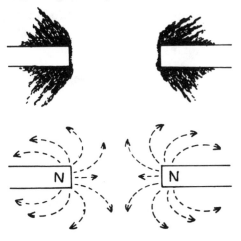

LUCKY ACCIDENTS

Scientists sometimes make some of their most important discoveries completely by accident. Or, they set out to prove one thing and wind up proving the opposite.

In the early part of the nineteenth century, scientists wanted to understand the relationship between magnetism and electricity, but they were nearly convinced that the two forces were not related. In 1820, the Danish doctor Hans Oersted was talking to his students about this subject when he accidentally moved an electric wire near a compass. The needle moved! An electrical current created a magnetic field before everyone's eyes — quite the opposite of what he was teaching that day!

A few years later, in England, Michael Faraday demonstrated the reverse — that a magnetic field produces electricity. His discovery led to the invention of the first electrical generator, the magnetic dynamo.

Scientists continue to study the odd relationship between electricity and magnetism. You could call these two forces cousins — alike in many ways, but very different, too. We already know that, unlike electricity, a magnetic field always flows into itself and can never separate from its poles. But another difference has to do with the fact that magnetism passes through many materials that do not conduct electricity. Glass and plastic are just two examples.

Electromagnets

Like permanent magnets, electromagnets have poles and magnetic fields. In fact, whenever electrical current passes through a wire, it produces a magnetic field around the wire. Every power line, appliance cord, electrical coil, and light bulb filament has a weak magnetic field surrounding it. But unlike a permanent magnet, you can reverse the direction of the current in an electromagnet, reversing the poles of the magnetic field.

MAGNETIC FIELD

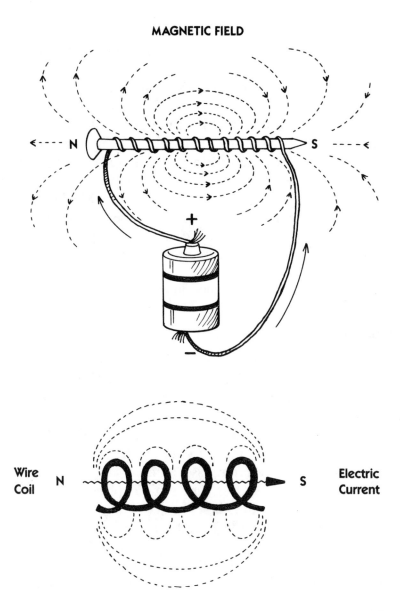

Wire Coil   N   S   Electric Current

Earth—the Biggest Magnet

The greatest electromagnet we know of is Earth. Most scientists think that the Earth's magnetism comes from huge electric currents deep in the Earth. They believe a region of molten iron surrounds the earth's solid core. The motion of the iron creates electricity, which in turn creates the magnetic field.

By studying old maps, scientists can trace changes in the Earth's magnetic field over the past 500 years. They can tell, for instance, that it grew weaker in this century. They also know that the poles drifted, and continue to drift, westward.

When scientists study the position of iron and magnetite particles in ancient clay banks, they find even more surprises. Like tiny compass needles frozen in time, the particles point to a north pole that no longer exists — close to what we now call the South Pole! So, many scientists now believe that the Earth's magnetic poles were once completely reversed.

Finding Our Way Around

Eight hundred years ago, the people of Europe didn't know much about the Earth's magnetism. But the Chinese were already using compasses by this time, and somebody finally brought one to Italy in about 1120. A hundred years later, sailors used the mysterious "dry needle," which always pointed north, to find their way around the Mediterranean.

We now depend on compasses for every kind of transportation. The compasses of supersonic airplanes use gyroscopes to steady them. These compasses also contain top-secret devices that actually make the compass more sensitive to the Earth's magnetic field.

Also, scientists now know the magnetic "north" is not the same as true north because the Earth's magnetic field does

TOPSY-TURVY

The following facts may surprise you. The needle of a compass is a magnet, and its north pole points towards the Earth's North Pole. But we know that like poles repel each other, and unlike poles attract each other. So how can a compass needle point north? The answer is that the magnetic *south pole* lies near the Earth's geographic *North Pole*, and the magnetic *north pole* lies near the Earth's geographic *South Pole*.

Navigators always use the direction north to figure out where they are. This is true even when they are so far from the North Pole that their compass needle barely reacts to it. But still the needle points north. Why? Because the farther they drift from the north pole, the closer they approach the south pole. When you use a compass below the equator, the Earth's magnetic north pole (in the south) has more influence on the needle than the magnetic South Pole (in the north). So although the needle continues to point towards the geographic north for a sailor travelling around, say, the tip of Africa, it's actually pulled to the closer pole in the geographic south.

This means that wherever you are on the face of the Earth, a good compass always points north!

not line up exactly with the geographic North and South poles. The difference, called *magnetic variation*, changes from place to place. Since local maps list these variations, navigators must pay careful attention to them.

Dips and Angles

To help sailors navigate, a compass should not only show the direction of a pole, but also its distance. A needle shows distance in how much it tilts, or dips, towards the ground.

Close to a pole, a needle stands practically on end because the pole pulls it sharply downwards. Near the equator, a needle hardly dips at all. As you can see, the dip of the needle traces the lines of the Earth's magnetic field.

Magnetic Field of Earth   **Dip of Compass Needle**

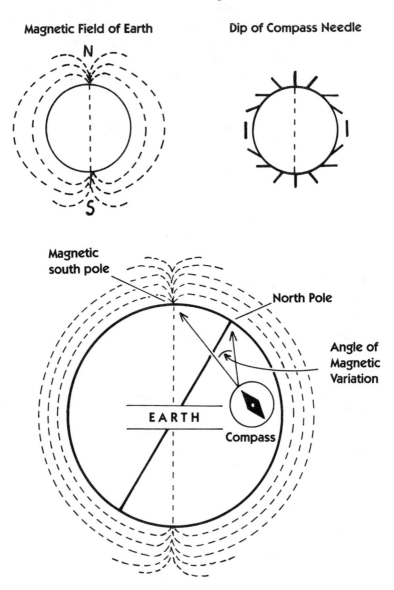

By measuring this angle of dip, navigators can figure out how far they are from either pole. But they need a special kind of instrument for this job: an *inclinometer*, or dip compass.

Think of an inclinometer as a compass turned on its side. But instead of showing north and south, an inclinometer shows the degrees of a circle. A long magnetized needle, attached to the center of the circle, indicates the angle of dip in degrees.

Although science has learned to use magnetism to drive powerful machines, navigate satellites, and carry our voices thousands of miles, if it weren't for the compass, we'd probably still be wandering all over the face of the Earth, hopelessly lost!

3. Magnets in Action

• •

Understanding magnetism means watching magnets at work. You may find, though, that the following experiments raise as many questions as answers. Don't get discouraged — that's what science is all about. The best scientists in the world have a lot to learn about mysterious magnetism!

Ghostly Dangers

A magnetic field can cause damage. In fact, you need to keep magnets away from such things as computers, tape recorders, answering machines, VCRs — any sensitive electronic device or appliance. By testing various materials against a magnet, we'll see if any of them provide protection from the potentially harmful effects of a magnetic field. Scientists call materials that shield electrical or magnetic forces *insulators*.

To do this experiment, you'll need a plastic ruler showing centimetres. You can also trace the ruler on the next page onto thin paper and glue the paper to cardboard.

JUST PASSING THROUGH

You Will Need
Plastic ruler showing
centimetres
Strong bar magnet
Shirt cardboard
Cellophane tape

One staple
Small, clear plastic bag
Piece of cloth
Piece of tissue paper
Microscope slide

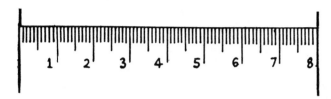

1. Place the ruler on a flat surface with the numbers facing you.
2. Put the north pole of the bar magnet just above the right edge of the ruler. Place the long side of one staple just above the left edge of the ruler.
3. Gradually slide the magnet along the ruler towards the staple. Notice at what point along the ruler the staple moves towards the magnet. Record the measurement.
4. Put the magnet in the plastic bag and slide it towards the staple again. Record the measurement. How do the two measurements compare?
5. Replace the plastic bag with cloth and repeat the procedure. Fold the tissue paper around the magnet. Finally, wrap the magnet's pole in aluminum foil. Record the measurements for each material and compare them.
6. Hold the glass microscope slide against the magnet's pole and test again, recording the measurement.

What Happened?

The plastic bag, cloth, and tissue paper don't block the effects of the magnet. The staple sticks to the magnet at about the same point along the scale for each material. The same holds true for the aluminum foil. As for the microscope slide, you probably had to move the magnet pretty close to the staple before anything happened. Magnetic lines of force pass through the slide but with less strength than before. This has to do with the thickness of the glass, not because glass makes a particularly good insulator.

So even though you tried many different kinds of material, none of them worked very well as an insulator.

Insulation Impossible

In fact, a strong magnetic field passes through everything! With no trouble at all, it flows through water, air, even a vacuum. None of the materials that protect against electricity does much about magnetism. But scientists have learned to trick magnetic lines of force in order to move them away from something or to contain them. They do this by using something magnets love — ferromagnetic metals.

As you already know, magnets prefer ferromagnetic metals to other materials. Ferromagnetic metals let the magnetic lines of force move through them very easily, so scientists say they have *low reluctance*. Other materials, such as paramagnetic metals, glass, ceramics, wood, water, and air, have *high reluctance*. Because magnetic lines of force take the path of least resistance, scientists can control their direction by drawing them into low reluctance areas.

For example, scientists use this trick in long cables that transmit electromagnetic signals. To keep the signals from leaking out of the cable and into the air, a tube of low reluctance metal surrounds the cable. The tube "catches" leaking signals and directs them back into the cable.

In the next experiment, you'll see another way to trick magnetic lines of force into unexpected places.

MAGNETISM—NOW YOU SEE IT . . .

You Will Need

 U-shaped magnet   *Flat steel cover from*
 Staples   *cooking pot*

1. Check to make sure the U-shaped magnet attracts the staples.

2. Check to make sure the magnet attracts the cooking pot cover.

3. Scatter the staples on a flat surface in an area no wider than the pot cover.

4. Place the magnet against the pot cover and slowly bring the cover down towards the staples.

What Happened?

With the magnet placed against the pot cover, you might expect the magnet's strength to pass through the cover and attract the staples. Instead, nothing happens. The magnetic lines of force travel into the cover and scatter outward to the edges. The cover acts as a "short circuit" to the lines of force. They prefer to scatter through the low-reluctance metal rather than extend into the high-reluctance air where they would attract the staples.

Fascinating Force Lines

The lines of force of magnetic fields are fascinating. With a strong magnet and some ferromagnetic objects, you can watch them work. The following projects use small ball bearings. They show how a magnetic field transforms other objects into magnets, changing the size of the original magnetic field.

STRING OF BEADS

You Will Need
   Bar magnet   *7 small ball bearings*

1. Lift a bar magnet by one pole so that the opposite pole points down. Pick up one of the ball bearings and bring it to the pole. The ball bearing sticks.
2. Add another ball bearing to the one that stuck to the magnet. Keep adding bearings until you have all seven hanging like a string of beads from the pole of the magnet.
3. Hold the top ball bearing with one hand and carefully pull the magnet away.

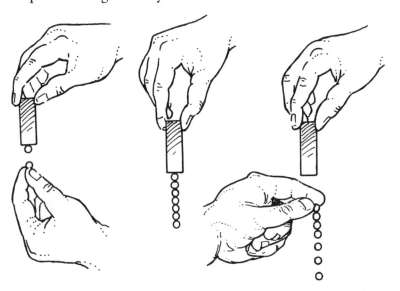

What Happened?
Each ball bearing becomes a magnet and holds the ball bearing below it. Each new ball bearing becomes part of the overall magnetic field and extends it downwards. When you pull the magnet away, the string of beads, still part of the

magnetic field, continue to stick together. As you move the magnet farther away, the ball bearings break away from the string, one by one.

KEEP APART, KEEP TOGETHER

You Will Need
Bar magnet   *7 small ball bearings*

1. If you haven't painted the poles of your magnet, place a compass against the ends to find the south pole (the needle will swing towards it).
2. At the south pole of the magnet, make a string of ball bearings. Use three ball bearings for each string. Notice how the strings push apart, particularly between the third ball bearing of each string.
3. Now attach one more ball bearing. The strings join together!

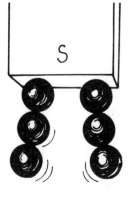 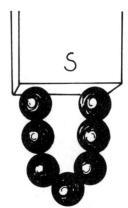

What Happened?
When you made two strings of three ball bearings, the unattached south poles of the third ball bearing on each string repelled each other. When you attached one more ball bearing, the strings joined together. Since the south poles of

the third ball bearings both attract the new ball bearing, they share the attraction by creating a magnetic field in the new ball bearing that has two north poles — one on each side!

Odd Effects

We've learned that you can fool magnetic lines of force, but you can never separate them from their poles. Lines of force also like to jump from object to object in order to become more concentrated. You can see this odd effect for yourself.

THE MAGIC THUMBTACK

You Will Need
    Bar magnet   *Steel nail*
    Thumbtack

1. Pick up the tack with a pole of the bar magnet. Turn the magnet sideways.

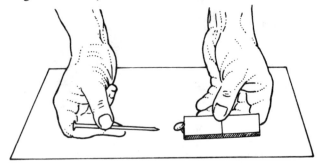

2. Slowly bring the point of the nail up to the tack, barely touching it.
3. Pull the nail away. The tack comes with it!

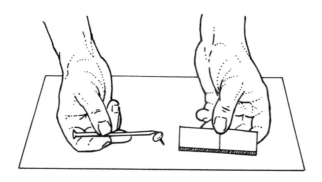

What Happened?

The magnetic field of the bar magnet passed into the nail, making the nail a stronger magnet. The thinner shape of the nail concentrated the magnetic lines of force.

TRICKS WITH RULERS

You Will Need

2 bar magnets   *2 metal rulers, same size*

1. Place a ruler against one magnet's north pole. Move the second magnet's north pole towards the ruler. Do the magnets attract or repel?
2. Repeat the procedure, but this time place a ruler against each north pole. What happens when you bring the two magnets together again?

What Happened?

The first time, both magnets stuck to the ruler, even though their north poles faced each other. The ruler allowed this to happen. Since the north poles of both magnets attracted the ruler, they shared the attraction by creating a magnetic field inside the ruler with two south poles, one on each side. Does this remind you of the two strings of beads?

If you reversed one of the magnets, they would still attract. The magnetic field of the ruler always adjusts to keep the magnets together.

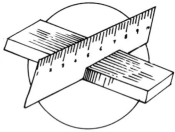

The second time, the magnets — each with its own ruler — pushed apart. Since they no longer had to share one ruler between them, their magnetic fields behaved in the more usual way.

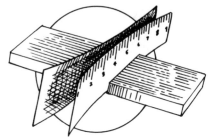

Metal Detectors

Learning how to use magnets and to manipulate magnetic fields leads scientists to make some of their most important breakthroughs. Take the metal detector, for instance. Since ferromagnetic metals become weakly magnetized by the Earth's magnetic field, scientists invented this instrument to find natural iron, nickel, or cobalt deposits.

Certain kinds of metal detector help military aircraft spot enemy submarines deep under water. Certain types of bombs look for a magnetic field to tell them when to explode. As we'll see later, this was a problem for large ships during World War II.

THE MAGNETIC FILTER

Metal detectors resemble another useful invention — the magnetic filter. Chemists use this to separate one material from another, particularly when the two materials are hard to tell apart. People who work in food processing factories know the danger of metal fragments winding up in our food. Farmers have the same concerns for their livestock, and so they invented something called a "cow magnet." This is a small, rounded magnet a cow swallows when it's just a calf. The magnet attracts sharp pieces of wire the cow might swallow while grazing and keeps the pieces from puncturing the cow's stomach. Amazing, but true!

RUST AND SAND

You Will Need

Rusty tin can   *Saucer*
File   *Fine sand*
Old teaspoon   *U-shaped magnet*
Sheet of paper   *Popsicle stick*

1. Use a file to scrape about a teaspoon of rust from the surface of the can onto a sheet of paper.
2. Using the back of the spoon, grind the rust into a fine powder.
3. Fold the paper and pour the powdered rust into a saucer.
4. Add two teaspoons of fine sand to the saucer.
5. Stir the sand and rust together until you have an evenly colored mixture.
6. Hold a magnet just above the saucer and gently push the mixture around with one end of a popsicle stick. Some of the rust particles jump from the sand onto the ends of the magnet.

7. Wipe the magnet clean and repeat the procedure until you separate all the particles of rust from the sand.

It's very useful to have magnets that separate metal particles from other materials. For example, some electric can openers have a round, magnetized blade. As the blade cuts through the lid, the magnet catches metal particles that might otherwise fall into the food.

Since we've talked about metal cans before, let's try an experiment with them. Remember, the Earth is a giant magnet with an enormous magnetic field. Remember, too, that powerful magnets can create other magnets out of ferromagnetic metals. Does this mean that every ferromagnetic object on the face of the Earth, including the cans in the cupboard, are magnets? Let's find out.

THE WORLD IN A TIN CAN

You Will Need
   2 soup cans   *Pocket compass*

1. Take two soup cans that have been sitting on the shelf for at least three days and place them on a flat surface, about 6 inches (15 cm) apart. Turn the second can upside down.

2. Hold a compass alongside the top of the first can and watch how the needle swings towards the can. Slowly move the compass down the can's side and notice how the needle swings away. By the time you reach the bottom, it points in the opposite direction. You've discovered a miniature magnetic field around the can, which is just like the Earth's magnetic field. Like the Earth, the can has a magnetic north and south pole and is actually a weak magnet.

3. Repeat this operation for the second upside-down can. Notice how the compass points south near the top and north near the bottom, in a mirror image of the first can. If you leave this can undisturbed for a few days, the Earth's magnetic field will remagnetize it, and the poles will reverse.

So to answer our question — yes, every ferromagnetic metal on the face of the earth is a weak magnet. You can make a simple test of this by holding your compass to the tops and bottoms of assorted metal objects to see if the needle swings. You'll find that the largest objects — refrigerators, safety vaults, lampposts, cars, even trailers — have magnetic fields. Stationary objects have stronger magnetic fields than moving ones.

4. Make It Work

• • • • • • • • • • • • • • •

The experiments in the previous chapter explored some basics about magnetism and electromagnetism. Now it's time to put those ideas to work. Building the projects in this chapter may convince you that we could hardly survive at all without magnets!

Compasses and Culture

The compass has played an important part in world history. It helped improve map-making and allowed explorers to chart and travel great stretches of sea that once terrified them. The compass also made trading routes possible. These routes led to an exchange of languages and ideas.

Building the following compass will give you a good idea of what an old-fashioned instrument looked like. Although a compass of this design performs well on a level surface, you'll also see why so many ships got lost!

WATER COMPASS

You Will Need
Shallow, glass pie dish
Piece of white cardboard,
  10 inches (25 cm)
  square
Piece of corkboard, 4
  inches (10 cm) square
Large paper clip
Bar magnet

Scissors
Thumbtack
String, 6 inches (15 cm)
  long
Rubber cement
Steel nut
Small wine glass
Marking pen

Making the Compass Card

1. Trace the bottom of the pie dish onto the cardboard and cut out the circle.

2. Use the marking pen to copy the compass card design.

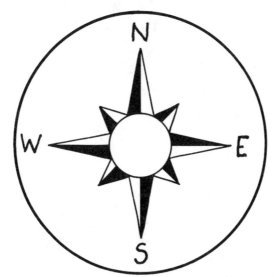

3. Place the compass card under the pie dish so that you can see it clearly through the glass.

Making the Floating Needle

1. Unbend the large paper clip until you have a straight piece of wire.

2. Use the north pole of the bar magnet to stroke the wire at least 50 times, from middle to end.

3. Turn the wire around and repeat the procedure, this time with the south pole of the bar magnet.

4. Test to make sure you have magnetized the wire by holding it against the thumbtack. If the attraction is weak, continue stroking.

5. Use the wine glass to trace a circle on the corkboard and cut it out.

6. With a little rubber cement, attach the wire to the center of the corkboard circle so that equal lengths of wire stick out from opposite sides.

7. Attach the thumbtack to the underside of the cork in the center of the circle.

8. Wrap one end of the string around the thumbtack and tie the other end to the nut.

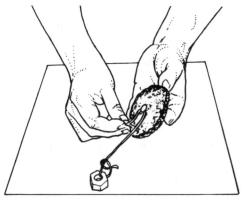

9. Carefully lift the cork and needle, with the nut dangling below, and place it in the center of the pie dish. Adjust the length of the string so that the nut just barely touches the bottom. The cork should float, keeping its upper surface dry. Allow a few minutes for your compass to stop bobbing around. Eventually the wire will settle into a north–south position and remain there. (It's not really cheating to test the accuracy of your compass by checking it against a store-bought compass).

10. Lift the pie dish and turn the compass card so that the *N* faces north, as indicated by the wire.

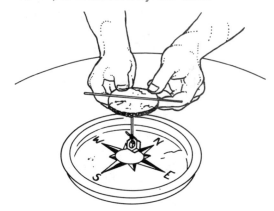

COMPASS HISTORY

The earliest compass was probably made from a piece of lodestone attached to the end of a wand. The wand was then hung so that the stone could swing freely, eventually pointing north. Such a primitive design wasn't very accurate, though, especially on a ship that was rolling on the high seas. Finally, someone discovered that a lodestone could magnetize a smaller and lighter piece of metal, creating a better compass.

The second improvement involved suspending the "needle" in a way that reduced friction. We know, from old descriptions of compasses, that most navigators wanted their needles hung from threads, though some preferred to float them in bowls of water. As metalworking improved, the style was to balance the needle on a carefully sharpened point.

But balanced or not, the dips and slants of a ship's deck still threw compasses out of whack. In the seventeenth century, a new idea came along — the gimbal ring. This handy little device surrounded the compass and kept it level, even on an unsteady surface. Now sailors could depend on compasses for accurate directions in all kinds of weather. The gimbal ring was such a good idea that we still use them on compasses today.

Finally, as compasses grew more accurate, navigators wanted more than the simple *cardinal points* — that is, North, South, East, and West — on the compass face. They wanted to know how *far* north they were going, for example. And so the compass circle was divided into 360 degrees — 90 degrees between each of the cardinal points.

Scientists use two types of compasses to study the earth's magnetic field: the *radial compass*, like the one above, and the inclinometer or *dip compass*.

Magnetic Treasure Box

By studying the Earth's magnetic field, scientists can collect important information in many areas. Geologists can find valuable mineral deposits underground by placing magnetometers aboard airplanes. These sensitive instruments point out odd "blips" in the Earth's magnetic field, which may indicate a deposit.

Another way to find deposits involves collecting soil samples and pushing magnets through them. This method actually permits geologists to sample some of the minerals that lie hidden, deep underground.

You can easily test the soil in your own back yard with the help of a strong U-shaped magnet.

SOIL SEPARATOR

You Will Need
Strong U-shaped magnet
String, 1 foot (30 cm) long
Plastic bag
Twist fastener

2 wide-mouthed glass jars
Garden spade
Soil
Wooden paint stirrer

1. Tie one end of the string around your U-magnet, making sure that the ends of the magnet point straight down.
2. Tie the free end of string around a pencil to make the magnet easier to lift.
3. Place the plastic bag over the magnet, pulling the bag tight across the ends. Use the twist fastener to close the bag.
4. Fill both jars about three-quarters full of clean water.

5. Place three spadefuls of soil in the first jar, stirring the soil and water mixture with the paint stirrer.

6. As the soil swirls through the water, dip the magnet into the jar, dropping it to the bottom and lifting it to the top again. Do this several times or until the soil begins to settle in the jar.

7. Carefully lift the magnet from the jar and look at the ends. Small grey, black, white, and red particles stick to the magnet through the plastic bag.

8. Dip the magnet into the second jar of clear water.

Carefully remove the plastic bag from the magnet so that the particles drop to the bottom of the jar.

9. Reattach the plastic bag and repeat this operation until your magnet no longer attracts particles from the soil and water. Carefully pour off the water from the jar containing the particles until you have just a little water remaining at the bottom.

10. Pour this remaining water and the particle mixture over a paper towel and let the towel dry. If possible, look at the dry particles under a microscope.

The particles belong in the class of metals called ferrites. Remember, ferrites are ferrimagnetic, and so they stick to a magnet. Your collection probably includes small quantities of magnetite (lodestone); manganese, magnesium, and zinc ferrites; barium and strontium ferrites; ferric oxide; and tiny amounts of such strange-sounding things as haematite, ilmenite, and yttrium-iron garnet (red particles). You can find small amounts of these metals in igneous (formed by heat) rocks, and you can be pretty sure that larger deposits exist close by.

Other Tools

Magnetism has always been important to navigators and geologists, who need tools like compasses and soil separators. The rest of us have more use for hammers, nails, and screwdrivers. But a magnet or two can make things much easier for us, too.

You've probably seen people struggling with screwdrivers. Maybe you've used one yourself. It's pretty hard to do a good job when you have to work in dark, hard-to-reach places. It's even harder when you're fighting gravity by trying to work a screw into an upper surface. Usually, the screw drops from its hole and disappears forever.

You can make the chore easier by magnetizing your screwdriver. This will make the screw stick to the flat end, or blade. You won't need to hold the screwdriver in one hand and the screw in the other hand anymore, which can be really helpful when you have to work in small areas.

MAGNETIZED SCREWDRIVER

You Will Need

Screwdriver   Strong bar magnet
Screw(s)

1. Stroke the shaft of your screwdriver at least 50 times in one direction with the pole of a bar magnet.
2. Test the magnetism by placing a screw in the blade and turning the screwdriver blade-up. If the screw falls out, keep stroking. Don't expect a really strong attraction. The screw should stick to the blade just enough to withstand a slight wiggle or two.

Here's another twist to an old idea. This one really comes in handy when you can't find a pad and pencil!

MAGNETIC MESSAGE BOARD

You Will Need
4 flat refrigerator
   magnets
$8^{1}/_{2} \times 11$-inch
   (22 × 28 cm) sheet of
   laminated paper

$2^{1}/_{2} \times 4$-inch (6 × 10 cm)
piece of cloth
Fine-tipped marking pen
   (water based)
Stapler
Rubber cement

You can find sheets of laminated paper in many craft shops. Some people use them for place mats on kitchen tables. If you have difficulty finding some, take an ordinary sheet of white paper and have it laminated. Most stationery or photography stores provide this inexpensive service.

1. Attach a refrigerator magnet to each corner of the laminated paper with rubber cement. Turn the paper over.

2. Place the piece of cloth on a flat surface and turn it so that the narrow side faces you. Fold it in half from the bottom, then fold it in half again.

3. Staple the top edge of the folded cloth against a narrow edge of the laminated paper. This will be the top of the message board, where the pen goes.

4. Stick the magnet side of the message board against the refrigerator. Slip the marking pen in the pen holder at the top edge.

5. Write something on your board to test it. Erase it, using a piece of moist paper towel or sponge.

Everyday Workhorse: The Electromagnet

We already know something about the strange relationship between electricity and magnetism. Remember how Hans

Oersted accidentally demonstrated how electricity produced magnetism, while Michael Faraday showed how magnets produced electricity? Both discoveries led to many important inventions. We'll re-create two of them.

When Oersted sent electricity through a piece of wire, he made a weak electromagnet. The compass needle moved towards the wire, proving it. In an earlier chapter, we built a simple electromagnet with a nail, copper wire, and battery. Like Oersted, we gave our electromagnet the compass test, sending electricity through the wire and proving that we'd made an electromagnet.

When Michael Faraday moved a magnet against a coil of wire, the compass needle also moved. But this time, it swung violently away from the wire — the way a compass behaves when electrical current is around. Faraday discovered something important: the principle of *induction*. The term means creating electricity in a conductor (any material that conducts electricity) by moving a magnet against it.

It was a dream come true! Imagine — electrical power made with ordinary magnets. Although no one quite understood how important electricity would become, Faraday knew he was on to something very big. In 1831, he built his first electric generator, the "Magnetic Dynamo."

We're building ours a bit later. It won't be nearly as complicated.

THE MAGNETIC DYNAMO

You Will Need
Bar magnet
5 feet (1.5 m) of insulated
  copper wire

Compass
Drinking glass
4 twist fasteners

1. Wrap the copper wire around a drinking glass, leaving about 18 inches (46 cm) of wire at the beginning and end. You should end up with a thick coil of wire around the glass.

2. Slide the coil from the glass and twist four fasteners around it. You want the coil thick, firmly bunched, and compact.

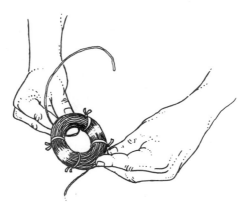

   To show the flow of electricity through the coil, you have to change the compass into something called a *galvanometer*, which will show the presence of an electrical current by moving the compass needle.
3. Wrap the free ends of wire around the compass in the same direction, connecting the wires.

4. With everything prepared, lift the coil with one hand and slowly move the bar magnet in and out of the coil's center.

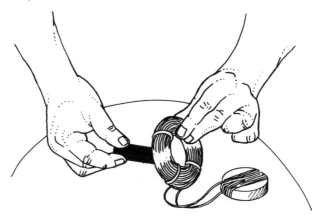

What Happens

Watch the compass needle — it jumps! Each time the magnet moves into the coil, the magnetic field creates an electrical current in the wire. Each time you remove the magnet, the current stops. Moving the magnet in and out of the coil produces a stream of electrical current we call *alternating current.*

Electricity and magnetism came together in another incredible invention that launched us into the Modern Age —

the electric motor. You can build this wonderful working model in an afternoon. The procedure is safe, and all the materials are easy to find.

SPOOL AND THREAD MOTOR

You Will Need

2 bar magnets
Large Styrofoam thread spool
Small Styrofoam thread spool
Styrofoam board, 11 × 14 × 1¼ inches (28 × 36 × 3 cm)
Two rubber bands
Piece of uninsulated (bare) copper wire, 5 feet (1.5 m) long

Piece of insulated (plastic-coated) copper wire, 4 feet (1.2 m) long
Aluminum or plastic knitting needle
4 large steel nails
2 small steel nails
2 thin copper strips
2 thumbtacks
6-volt battery
Paper clip
Scissors

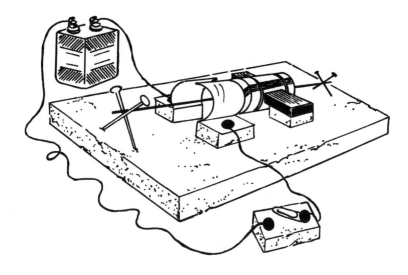

Sum of the Parts

A simple motor has five important parts: a moving *armature*, stationary *field magnets*, a *commutator*, a *power source*, and a *switch*.

In this case, of course, the 6-volt battery provides the power. The armature connects to the battery so that current flows into the coil and creates an electromagnetic field around it. The stationary field magnets surround the armature with a magnetic field of their own. The commutator acts as a switch. It turns the current flowing through the armature on and off. These parts work together to operate the motor.

Making the Armature

1. Hold the large spool horizontally and wrap the 5-foot (1.5 m) piece of bare copper wire around it about 20 times, leaving at least 3 inches (7.6 cm) of loose wire at both ends.

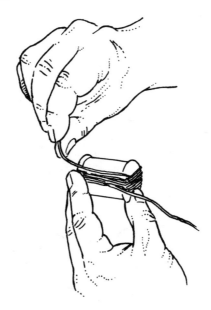

2. Turn the spool on its end. Push two small nails into the top of the spool, on opposite sides of the coil, and wrap one end of the wire around each of them. These "terminal nails" are the beginning of the commutator mechanism.

3. Secure the coil by wrapping the rubber bands around the top and bottom edges of the spool. Push the knitting needle halfway through the center hole of the spool, forcing it through the coil.

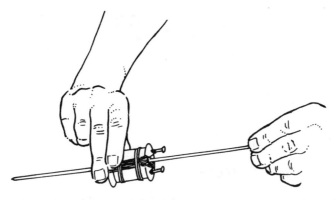

4. Use the scissors to cut the Styrofoam board into a rectangular base 7 × 14 inches (18 cm × 36 cm). From the extra piece, cut out a rectangle 1 × 1½ inch (2.5 cm × 3.8 cm). Later, you'll use this smaller piece to make the simple open/close switch.

5. Take a pair of large nails and push them into the narrow side of the base so that they make an *X*. At the other side, make another *X* with the second pair of nails.

6. Place the knitting needle across these *X*s. To keep the needle from slipping to the side as it turns, put two small bands of tape on opposite sides of the needle where it rests on the *X*s.

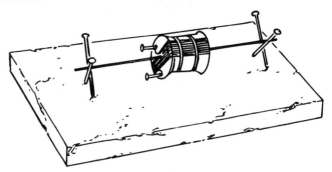

Making the Commutator

1. Fold each copper strip in half. Unfold the strips, but do not flatten them out again. You want each strip in the shape of a right angle.

2. Bend one half of each strip around the smaller spool, forming it into an even curve. Remove the spool. Each strip should now have a flat half and a curved half.

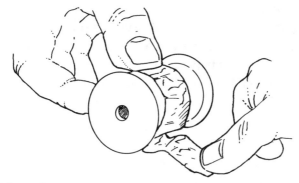

3. Place the strips on opposite sides of the knitting needle so that the curved halves of the strips trace a broken "*O*" around the contact nails protruding from the larger spool. Push a tack through the flat halves of the strips to secure them to the base.

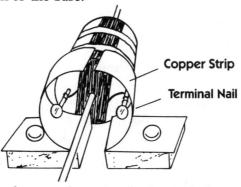

Copper Strip

Terminal Nail

4. Check to make sure the strips don't touch the spool, or each other, and that the split down the *O*'s center is just a little wider than a contact nail. The contact nails should brush against the curving strips as the armature turns.

Making the Field Magnets and Switch

1. Place the bar magnets on opposite sides of the spool, opposite poles of the magnets facing each other. Make sure the pole of each magnet lies no more than 1 inch (2.5 cm) from the side of the spool.

2. To complete the open/close switch, take the 1 × 1½-inch (2.5 × 3.8 cm) piece of Styrofoam board and push thumbtacks into the narrow sides of it. One of the tacks will fasten down a paper clip. The paper clip should pivot so it can touch the other "contact" tack, closing the switch.

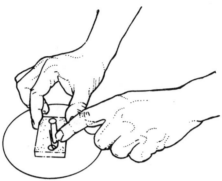

Making Connections

Now it's time to connect the motor to the battery and switch.
1. Cut the 4-foot (1.2 m) piece of insulated wire into two 1-foot (30 cm) sections and one 2-foot (60 m) section.
2. Hold any one of the sections ½ inch (1.2 cm) from the end and partially cut through the wire with the scissors. Your cut should be just deep enough to go through the plastic coating.

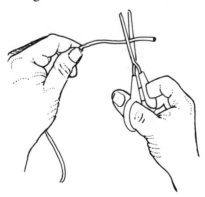

3. Pull the plastic coating off, exposing the bare wire. Repeat this for the remaining sections.

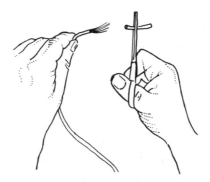

4. Take the 1-foot (30 cm) sections and attach one end of each to the tacks holding the copper strips. Of the three sections of copper wire, the two 1-foot (30 cm) sections are attached to the copper strips of the commutator, and the one 2-foot (60 cm) section remains unattached.

5. Take the other end of each 1-foot (30 cm) section and twist it around the paper clip and battery terminal, respectively.

6. Connect the 2-foot (60 cm) piece of wire to the contact tack of the switch and to the battery terminal.

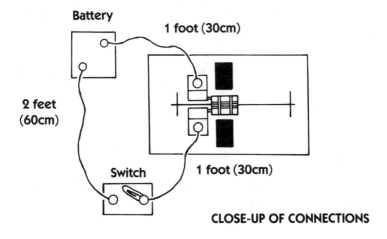

CLOSE-UP OF CONNECTIONS

7. Turn the spool so that the armature coil sits upright. Close the switch by sliding the paper clip against its pivot tack until the top of the clip makes contact with the second tack. If nothing happens, give the spool a slight nudge. Your motor will begin spinning.

How It Works

Since magnetic fields never separate from their poles, they can push and twist each other around, but never combine. A motor works because the electromagnetic field of the armature coil and the magnetic field of the bar magnets push and twist to produce a turning motion.

When you close the switch, the current flows in one direction from the battery into one of the brass strips of the commutator, then through one of the contact nails into the armature coil. It leaves the coil through the other contact nail, flowing out through the commutator's second brass strip and back into the battery.

Electrical current, flowing in one direction through the armature coil, creates an electromagnetic field around the coil with poles on opposite sides of the spool. Remember, opposite poles attract and like poles repel, so the spool begins to rotate until its poles lie against the corresponding opposite poles of the bar magnets.

But what makes it spin? Once the poles of the armature coil and bar magnets line up so that unlike poles face each other, you wouldn't expect further movement. But something happens to keep things going.

Commuting Current

The electromagnetic field surrounding the armature lasts only as along as both contact nails touch the brass strips of the commutator. This field has a north pole at one end and a south pole at the other, depending on the current's direction. The position of these poles causes the armature to rotate, so that its poles lie against the corresponding opposite poles of the bar magnets.

Starting from an upright position, the poles of the armature coil push away from like poles and move towards unlike poles on the bar magnets. But as the armature makes a quarter turn, the contact nails move into the split between the brass strips, briefly stopping the flow of current through the coil. As the momentum-driven armature continues to rotate another quarter turn, the nails touch the brass strips again, and the flow of current continues. By this time, though, the armature has "flipped" a half-circle, so what started out as the armature's north pole against the bar magnets' south pole, now becomes the armature's south pole against the magnets' south pole.

Repelled by like pole against like pole again, the armature rotates another half-circle, only to have its poles reverse *again*. And so the rotation continues.

5. Games, Tricks and Toys

· ·

This chapter describes a few ways to have fun with magnets.
Some of the most important early discoveries in magnetism
probably came from building toys or playing games.

Strange Effects

You've probably seen or heard of the magician's trick where a
lady floats, or "levitates," in midair. In the next two projects,
we'll use the magnetic forces of attraction and repulsion to
create similar effects.

LEVITATING LADIES

You Will Need

    5 bar magnets
    6 sharpened pencils
    Marking pen

    Styrofoam board
      4 × 6 × 1¼ inches
      (10 × 15 × 3 cm)
      White correction fluid

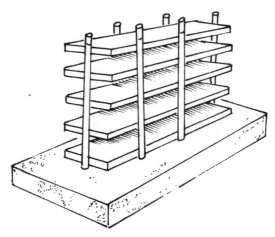

1. Put the Styrofoam board on a flat surface with one of the long sides facing you. Place the bar magnet in the center of the board, facing the same way.

2. Use the marking pen to trace six points against the bar magnet — two points along each side edge and one point in the center of each end.

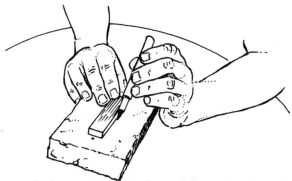

3. Remove the bar magnet and carefully push the points of the six pencils into the holes. You'll have a brace just large enough to contain the magnets. If the brace spreads open at the top, reinforce the pencils by looping a piece of cellophane tape around the ends of the erasers.

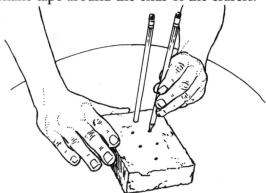

4. Take the magnets and figure out how to stack them so that the top surface of a magnet always repulses the bottom surface of the magnet above it.

5. Use a compass to identify the north and south sides of each magnet. Move each magnet towards the north-

pointing compass needle. When the needle swings away, it is indicating the north side of the magnet. When the needle swings towards the magnet, it is indicating the south side. Mark the north side of each magnet with a small dab of white correction fluid.

6. Slide the first bar magnet into the brace so that it rests, north side down, against the Styrofoam board. Put the second magnet, south side down, into the brace. Since the south sides of both magnets face each other, and since like poles repel, the second magnet floats above the first magnet!

7. Place a third magnet, north side down, over the second magnet. Add the fourth and fifth magnets in the same arrangement. The fifth magnet, placed north side down, floats over the fourth magnet and completes the stack. You now have four magnets floating in midair!

Scientists have long known that the force of magnetism is stronger than the force of gravity. By sticking fast to the side of a refrigerator, even a small magnet thumbs its nose at the mighty pull of the Earth. In this project, the force of repulsion was enough to keep magnets floating above each other.

Push down on the top magnet and notice the cushion effect. Magnets stacked this way can support a considerable amount of weight.

FLYING PAPER CLIP

You Will Need

*Wooden dowel, about 10
  inches (25 cm) long*
Bar magnet
Handkerchief
*Piece of thread, 14 inches
  (36 cm) long*

*Piece of string, 6 inches
  (15 cm) long*
2 rubber bands
Paper clip
Cellophane tape

You can impress your friends with this magnetic magic-wand trick. As you wave your wand over a paper clip, the clip springs to life, attracted to the tip of the wand but never touching it. As you raise the wand in the air, the paper clip follows, until it floats like a kite at the end of its string. A twist of your wand breaks the spell.

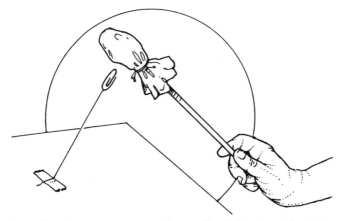

1. Attach a bar magnet to the end of the dowel with two rubber bands.

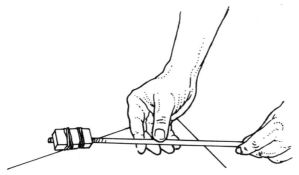

2. Cover the magnet end of the dowel with the hand-kerchief. Tie the piece of string around the handkerchief to keep it in place. If you're using an old handkerchief, you may want to trim it so that you cover just the top of the dowel and the magnet.
3. Tie one end of the long piece of thread to the paper clip.

Attach the other end of the thread to the top of the table with a little tape. Pull the clip to straighten the thread.

4. Bring the magnet end of your wand against the paper clip. When the clip sticks to the magnet, slowly move the wand about ½ inch (1.2 cm) away. The paper clip will appear to float in midair as it follows the magnet without actually touching it.

5. Slowly raise the wand, and the clip will follow. Do some loops and figure eights for an extra special performance. When you want the show to end, break the attraction by rotating your wrist, twisting the wand.

Magnetic Games

Small, permanent magnets can help you create some fun games. Adding magnets to an old favorite, such as checkers, allows you to take the game with you on car trips.

MAGNETIC CHECKERS

You Will Need
Square tin cookie-box
   cover
32 washers, 1⅝ inches
   (4 cm) in diameter

Bar magnet
Permanent marking pen
Ruler
Red and black enamel

Making the Board and Pieces

1. Turn the cookie-box cover upside down and place it on a flat surface. Use a ruler to measure the bottom edge of the cover. Divide that measurement by 8. For example, if the cover is 12 inches (30 cm) square, dividing the bottom edge by 8 gives you 1½-inch (3.8 cm) spaces. If the cover is 10 inches (25 cm) square, dividing the bottom edge by 8 gives you 1¼-inch (3 cm) spaces.

2. Mark the bottom edge into 8 equal sections. Draw lines from the bottom edge to the top edge so that you have eight columns.
3. Rotate the cover a quarter turn and repeat Steps 1 and 2. You'll wind up with a checkerboard design of 64 squares.
4. Paint the square in the left corner black. Leave the square above it and to the right of it unpainted. Paint the square diagonally to the right black, also. Continue painting alternate squares until you have 32 black squares. Allow the paint to dry before painting the remaining 32 squares red.
5. To make checker pieces, spread out some newspaper and divide the washers into two groups of 12. Paint the first group red and the second group black. You only need to paint one side of the washers. Allow the paint to dry.
6. Magnetize the washers by stroking a pole of the bar magnet over their unpainted sides. Test each washer to make sure it sticks firmly to the checkerboard.

MAGNETIC HOCKEY

Magnetic hockey captures some of the excitement of the original game on your table.

You Will Need
Poster board, 11 × 17
    inches (28 × 43 cm)
2 index cards, 3 × 5
    inches (7.6 × 12.7 cm)
2 washers
Small plastic button
Scissors
Ruler

Marking pen
Masking tape
4 rubber bands
4 paper cups
2 paint stirrers
2 bar magnets
Red and blue paint

Court, Puck, and Players

1. Place the poster board on a flat surface with one of the long sides facing you. Draw the playing court design with the marking pen. Use a saucer to trace the circle in the middle.

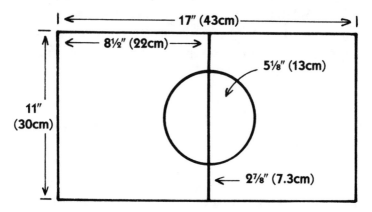

2. Make a fence so that the puck doesn't fly off the playing court during a game. The fence also keeps the court from sagging when you place it over the paper cups. Turn the poster board over so that the blank side faces you. Draw lines parallel to, and ½ inch (1.2 cm) from, all four edges of the poster board.

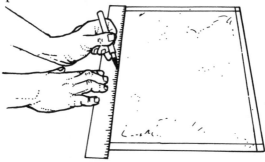

3. Cut out the corners of the poster board where the lines connect. Flip the poster board over and carefully bend along these lines until you have a fence.

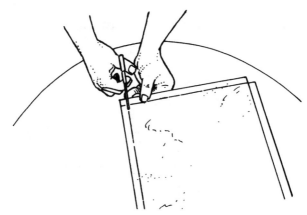

Connect the corners of the fence with tape.

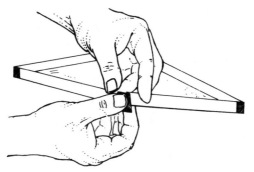

4. For your goal nets, trace the following pattern on the index cards. Fold along the dotted lines.

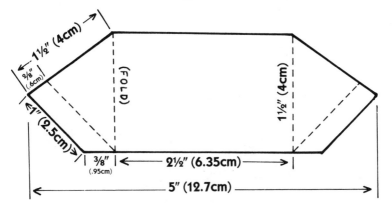

Attach the nets along the flaps with masking tape.

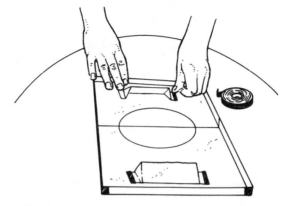

5. To make the hockey players, one blue and one red, paint just one side of each washer. The plastic button makes a good puck.

6. For the wands, attach the bar magnets to the ends of the paint stirrers so that a pole of each magnet sticks out from the end. Secure the magnets in place with rubber bands. A player moves when you place a magnet under the board, directly beneath the washer.

7. Turn the paper cups upside down and rest a corner of the poster board on each cup, taping the poster board in place. To keep it from moving during a fast-paced game, attach the cups to the table with some strips of masking tape.

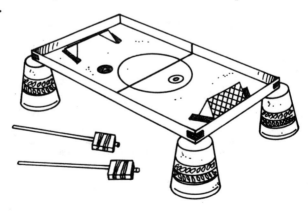

Playing Magnetic Hockey

Each game lasts 10 minutes. Place the puck in the middle of the circle, on the line. The washer-players rest at opposite sides of the puck, also in the circle. At the signal, the players attempt to slam the puck into the opponent's goal net. Each player tries to block the other's move. A player scores 1 point each time he hits a puck into the opponent's net. After 10 minutes, the player with the most points wins the game.

PITCHING WASHERS

Pitching washers might remind you a little of darts. But here, you won't have to worry about poking holes in the walls, floor, or ceiling!

You Will Need

*Large steel mixing bowl
or wok
Grease pencil*

*10 washers
Red and blue paint
Bar magnet*

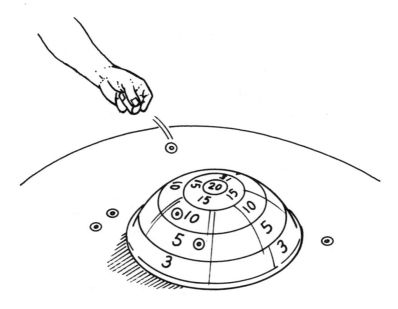

Bowl, Board, and Pieces

1. Turn the mixing bowl or wok so that the hollow side faces down. Use the grease pencil to mark the bowl according to the diagram. The placement of numbers reflects the difficulty in keeping a washer attached to that part of the bowl.

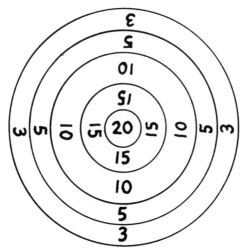

2. Divide the 10 washers into two groups of five. Paint both sides of the first group red and both sides of the second group blue. Allow the paint to dry.
3. Magnetize each washer by stroking one side with a pole of the bar magnet. Test each washer's attraction to the surface of the bowl.

Pitching for Points

Players stand five feet (1.5 m) from the bowl and take turns pitching washers for points. If a player misses the bowl, he loses the next turn. When players run out of washers, the one with the highest score wins the game.

When you finish the game, use a washcloth, warm water, and a little soap to remove the grease pencil from the bowl.

GONE FISHIN'

You Will Need

Plastic washtub or basin
Blue poster paint
Flour
Plastic bag
Hole punch
8 paper clips
2 small horseshoe magnets

String
Two 3-foot (.9 m) bamboo
  poles (available in
  gardening or hardware
  stores)
Wooden spoon

Fishing Basics

1. Fill the washtub with water and add just enough blue paint to tint the water. Add about 2 cups (.48 l) of flour. Use the wooden spoon to stir the water until the paint and flour completely dissolve.
2. Cut seven small fish in various sizes from the plastic bag. Start with some small fish first, making each one about 2 inches (5 cm) long. The largest fish should be no more than 5 inches (12.7 cm) long.

3. Arrange your fish in order of increasing size. Punch one hole in the center of the smallest fish. Punch two holes in the center of the next-to-smallest fish. Punch three holes in the fish after that, and so on, until you've punched seven holes in the largest fish. Each hole counts for a point. (The largest fish has the most points.)

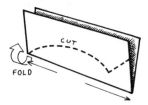 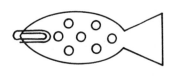

4. Cut out an "old tire," a hollow circle 3 inches (7.6 cm) in diameter, from the remaining piece of plastic bag. Attach a paper clip to the front of each fish and to the tire.

5. Throw the fish and the tire into the washtub, making sure everything sinks and disappears in the cloudy water.

6. Make fishing rods by tying 3 feet (.9 m) of string to the end of each bamboo pole. Tie the horseshoe magnets to the ends of the strings.

Playing the Game

Players take turns fishing. Before the first player starts fishing, the second player stirs the water with the wooden spoon. The first player dips his rod into the water and pulls it out again quickly, either catching a fish, several fish, or nothing at all. If he catches a fish, he receives the point value for the fish. If he catches two fish, he gets points for each fish. If he catches the tire, he loses a turn (if he has no fish) or throws back whatever fish he's caught up to that point. He then throws the tire back in the water.

Players take turns until no fish are left in the tub. The player with the most points wins.

MODEL CAR RACE

You Will Need

White poster board,
  2 × 3 feet (.6 × .9 m)
Marking pen
2 thumbtacks
2 bar magnets
Corkboard
2 paint stirrers

4 rubber bands
Rubber cement
4 paper cups
Masking tape
2 small plastic or wooden
  cars, same size

Road and Track

1. Copy the divided-track design onto the poster board. You can come up with your own design if you like, but make sure the ends of the track are at opposite corners of the poster board.

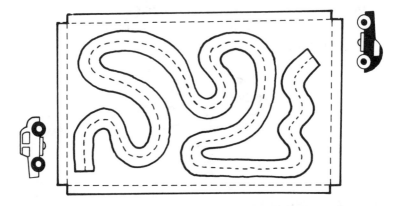

2. To keep the poster board from sagging when you place it on the cups, bend each edge of the board until you have a fence about ½ inch (1.2 cm) tall. Tape the corners of the fence together. (See the illustrations on page 81.)

3. Turn four paper cups upside down and arrange them in a rectangle. Flip the poster board over and rest each corner on a paper cup, moving the cups when necessary. Tape the corners of the poster board to the cups. You should now have a sturdy surface on which to race your cars.

4. Depending on the kind of car you have, you may have to fix the underpart of the model so that the thumbtack sits against the poster board. If you have a wooden car, turn the car over and press the thumbtack directly into the wood, towards the car's front end. If the tack doesn't protrude far enough to touch the poster board, glue a small piece of corkboard to the car's underside and press the tack into the cork. If you have a plastic car with a hollow interior, cut a piece of cork large enough to wedge inside. Secure the piece with some glue and press in a tack.

5. To make the first wand, attach a bar magnet to the end of a paint stirrer with two rubber bands. Make sure one of the poles protrudes about an inch (2.5 cm) from the end of the stick. Flip the stick over to make certain the magnet remains firmly attached. Repeat the procedure for the second wand.

Start Your Engines

On your track, notice that the starting line for one car becomes the finish line for the other car. Racers position their cars at opposite corners of the poster board. At a given signal, they place their wands under their cars and pull them along the track in opposite directions. The first car to cross a finish line wins the race.

Magnetic Toys

The following projects may seem familiar to you. The magical effect depends on carefully placing the magnets. Use your imagination to invent some toys of your own.

FIGURE SKATER ON MIRROR LAKE

You Will Need

Mirror, 8 × 5 inches
(20 × 12.7 cm)
Paint stirrer
Bar magnet
Small, round magnet
2 rubber bands
Construction paper

Rubber cement
Marking pen
Scissors
Cellophane tape
Ruler
Talcum powder

Skater, Wand, and Lake

1. Cut a 1 × 4¾-inch (2.5 × 12 cm) strip from a light-colored piece of construction paper. Hold the strip with one of the narrow sides facing you and measure 2 inches

(5 cm) down from the top edge. Fold the paper to the 2-inch (5 cm) mark so that you have a ¾-inch (2 cm) piece sticking out from the bottom.

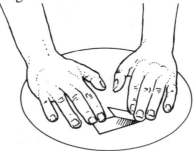

Fold this ¾-inch (2 cm) piece over the strip, then straighten it out again.

2. Copy the figure skater drawing on one side of the folded strip. Turn the strip so that the folded side faces you. Carefully cut around the figure skater — actually *two* figure skaters, one on each side of the strip — but leave the heads joined.

3. Refold and tape the ¾-inch (2 cm) piece so it forms a base and connects the two figure skaters. Glue the round magnet to the base between the two skaters.

4. For the wand, attach the bar magnet to the end of the paint stirrer with the two rubber bands. Make sure one of the poles protrudes about 1 inch (2.5 cm) from the end of the stick. Flip the stick over to make sure the magnet doesn't drop off.

5. To make the lake, put the mirror on two pieces of 2 × 4-inch (5 × 10 cm) wood or between two books. Make sure the area under the mirror is clear.

6. Sprinkle a little talcum powder over the mirror to give it an icy look. The dusting will also allow you to see the tracks your figure skater makes as she glides over the surface of the lake.

Crazy Eights

Place the figure skater on the lake and move the magnet side of the wand under the mirror until the magnet's pole lies directly beneath the figure. The magnet will either attract or repel the skater. If attracted, the skater glides over the surface of the lake, pulled forward by your wand. If repelled, the skater spins, twists and wobbles.

You can get your skater to do some crazy skating by rapidly flipping the wand over and over.

MAGNETIC TUGBOATS

You Will Need

2 pieces of corkboard or
   Styrofoam
Construction paper
2 small, round corks
10 thumbtacks
2 paper clips
Scissors
2 small horseshoe magnets

2 bamboo poles, 24 inches
   (60 cm) long (available
   in gardening or
   hardware stores)
String
Rubber cement
Plastic washtub or basin

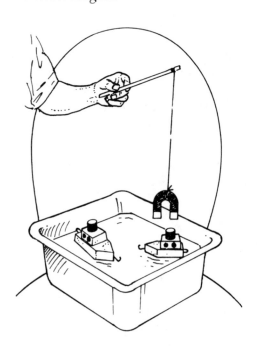

Boats and Rods

1. Cut the corkboard or Styrofoam into two small boat shapes. Cut a smaller rectangle to glue on top of the boat shapes. Top off the boats with small cork "smokestacks."

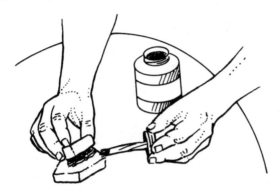

2. Push three thumbtacks into each boat: one tack at the top of the cork and two on opposite sides of it.

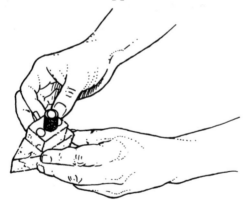

3. Straighten the four paper clips. Shape the first two into small hooks and the second two into U-shapes. Push a hook into the tip of each boat and the U-shape into the back. You can finish your boats with enamel paint, covering the tacks on the deck side and adding such details as portholes and deck stripes.

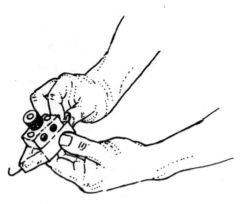

4. To make the rods, cut two 12-inch (30 cm) pieces of string and tie one end of each to the horseshoe magnets. Tie the free ends of the string to the bamboo poles. You should now have two fishing rods with magnets instead of hooks.

5. Fill the washtub with water and float your tugboats. You and a friend can then maneuver your boats by suspending the horseshoe magnets over them and moving the rods. Test your skill by maneuvering the boats so that they link together and one tugs the other along.

6. Magnets and Modern Science

● ●

We've seen magnets in various shapes, sizes, and designs. We've looked at some of the ways they function as tools and machines. We've used magnets in toys and games and enjoyed some of the unusual "special effects" they can produce. But scientists discover new things about magnetism every day, and this chapter will look at some of the ways they plan to use those discoveries. Many of these ideas are still "on the drawing boards," others have already found their ways into such fields as astronomy, medicine, engineering, and nuclear science.

The Eagle Has Landed

On the 20th of July, 1969, a crew of three astronauts landed on the Moon. Their journey lasted 4 days, 6 hours, 45 minutes, and 40 seconds. When they blasted off, their spacecraft was on the side of the Earth not facing the Moon. To complicate things, the Moon was circling the Earth. And if that weren't enough, the Earth, too, was spinning — at 1,600 miles (2,575 km) per hour!

Making sure the astronauts landed where they were supposed to — or landed *at all* — was the toughest navigational problem scientists had ever tried to solve. But the *Eagle* landed just a little over a mile from its target point.

The hero in this amazing adventure was a magnetic instrument called an *accelerometer*. It fed important information to computers which, in turn, fired the engines if the spacecraft was drifting off course. How did the computers know? The accelerometer compared where the spacecraft was, to where it was *supposed* to be, by measuring tiny changes in its direction.

An accelerometer contains a chamber about the size of a shoe box. Inside the chamber is a small metal sphere surrounded by liquid. To keep the sphere from drifting aimlessly in a weightless environment, powerful electromagnets surround the chamber and hold the sphere at the exact center.

If the chamber changes direction, as it would if the spacecraft began to drift off course, the metal sphere moves away from the center. The electromagnets measure how much the sphere has moved and tell the spacecraft's computers to fire or switch off certain engines. This gets the spacecraft back on course.

Jacob's Ladder

Since the Moon landing, scientists have looked for ways to make space exploration less expensive. A flight of the shuttle, for instance, costs nearly $500 million! And much of the expense burns up, since the costliest part involves the huge amount of fuel needed to escape Earth's gravity.

In the not-too-distant future, scientists from many nations may build a permanent space station. This station will not orbit the Earth like a satellite, but move along with the Earth's rotation. Scientists call this type of space motion *geocentric.*

A space station will have many advantages for future astronauts. It will provide a convenient place to stop, refuel, and load supplies before a longer voyage. Larger space stations may even build and launch spacecrafts outside the Earth's gravity, saving billions of dollars in fuel. But one problem still bothers scientists. Building a space station means getting a huge amount of construction material into space. How will they get it all up there?

Jacob's Ladder is one of the more unusual ideas. In the Bible, Jacob dreamt of a long ladder reaching into heaven. Space scientists dream of a huge steel cable, anchored to Earth on one end, and to a geocentric space station core on the other end. A powerful electromagnet elevator would climb the cable carrying construction materials clear into space!

You can see that this type of electromagnet would have to be extremely powerful and lightweight. Scientists hope to build such magnets in the future from superconducting rare earth metals. More about that later.

Stuff of the Universe

The space shuttle has allowed scientists to perform many experiments in a weightless environment. The matter in deep space — interstellar particles, magnetic meteors, and cosmic rays — interests them very much. But you don't have to ride the shuttle to gather samples of deep space material for yourself. Particles enter our atmosphere every second, many drifting to Earth. With the help of magnets, we can find some of them, especially the micrometeorites.

Unlike ordinary meteors, micrometeorites are too small and too light to burn up as they enter the Earth's atmosphere. Most float in the air, falling to the ground only when they stick to tiny droplets of water or dust particles. Like larger meteorites, though, micrometeorites can be either metallic or rocky and are mostly made up of materials left by comets and the explosions of stars.

Look for micrometeorites shortly after a major meteor shower. The best showers, Perseids and Geminids, reach their peaks on August 11 and December 13 every year. Plan to carry out the first phase of your project, collecting rainwater, around these dates.

MICROMETEORITE COLLECTING

You Will Need
2 Pyrex pie dishes
1 quart (.9 l) distilled
  water
Horseshoe magnet
Sewing needle
Clear plastic bag

Hot plate
Disposable eyedropper
2 microscope slides
Microscope or magnifying
  glass

Magnet Sweep for Particles
1. Wash the two Pyrex pie dishes thoroughly with soap and water to remove dust particles.
2. Leave the first dish outside for a few days to collect rainwater. If you live in an area where it doesn't rain much, fill the dish with distilled water and leave it outside for at least a week.

3. After enough rainwater collects, or the water-filled dish has been left undisturbed for a while, cover the horseshoe magnet with the clear plastic bag and place it in the dish. Slowly sweep the poles of the magnet along the bottom and sides of the dish. Because some micrometeorites are ferromagnetic, the magnet will attract them.

4. Fill the second dish with distilled water.

5. Carefully remove the magnet from the first dish and place it in the second dish.

6. Remove the bag from the magnet and gently swirl it around to allow the micrometeorites to fall to the bottom of the dish.

7. Ask an adult for help if you've never used a hot plate before. Evaporate the distilled water from the second dish so that you can collect the ferromagnetic micrometeorites. To do this, place the dish on the hot plate, switch the hot plate on, and allow the water to boil away completely. Be very cautious during this part of the experiment — the hot plate, the Pyrex dish, and the water will all become very hot. When the water boils away, immediately turn off the hot plate and wait half an hour for the dish to cool.

8. Magnetize the sewing needle by rubbing it at least 50 times in one direction against a pole of the horseshoe magnet. Drag the magnetized needle against the bottom and sides of the second dish.

9. Carefully tap the needle onto a clean microscope slide.

Observing the Micrometeorites

1. Go back to the first dish again. Place the dish on the hot plate and evaporate the water. Allow the dish to cool.

2. Scrape the bottom and sides of the dish with the needle. Carefully tip the dish on its side so that the loosened debris falls onto the microscope side.

3. Observe the particles on your slide with a microscope or magnifying glass. If you use a magnifying glass, place the slide on a white piece of paper.

What You See

Scientists classify micrometeorites in four main groups. Only the first group, *siderites*, stick firmly to magnets. Siderites are ferromagnetic. They consist of 92 percent iron, 7 percent nickel, and a trace of cobalt. They appear round and

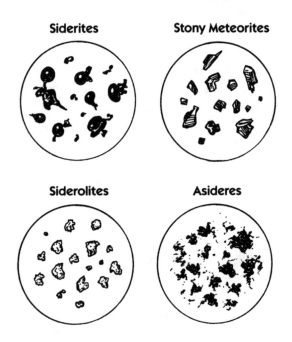

Siderites

Stony Meteorites

Siderolites

Asideres

droplet-shaped on your slide. These shapes show the enormous heat from an exploding star.

The micrometeorites of the second group, *stony meteorites*, do not stick to magnets. They consist mostly of silica and magnesium oxides. These have irregular shapes.

The micrometeorites of the third group, *siderolites*, contain minerals and ferrimagnetic metals. Magnets attract them, but only weakly. These look like cinders on your slide.

Asideres, the fourth group, look like tiny sponges and contain no ferrous material at all.

Magnets and Modern Engineering

Learning new things about magnetism makes it possible to improve old ideas and to invent new ones, especially in the area of transportation. Trains of the future may have "frictionless" electromagnets instead of wheels. Cars, buses, and trucks may ride on a cushion of electromagnets. As for buildings, electromagnetic "earthquake springs" just might make things a little safer for the people living or working inside them.

When scientists use the force of repulsion between magnets to lift or cushion a heavy object, they call it *magnetic suspension*. You can test this yourself with the following project.

FLOATING PLATFORM

You Will Need
20 ring magnets
4 sharpened pencils
Styrofoam, 5 × 5 × 1½
  inches (12.7 × 12.7
  × 3.8 cm)

Styrofoam, 5 × 5 × ⅛
  inches (12.7 × 12.7
  × .3 cm)
White correction fluid

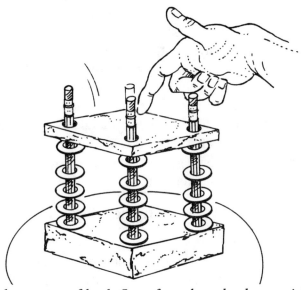

1. In the center of both Styrofoam boards, draw a 4-inch (10 cm) square.
2. Take the thinner piece of Styrofoam board and carefully push a pencil through each corner of the square you just measured. Be sure to make the holes wide enough for the pencil to slip through easily.
3. Take the thicker piece of Styrofoam board and push a pencil into each of the corners of the measured square. The pencils should stand straight up and not wobble.
4. Divide the ring magnets into four groups of five. For each group, figure out how to stack the magnets so that the top surface of a magnet always repulses the bottom surface of the magnet above it. If you haven't painted the poles of the magnets, you'll need a compass to identify north and south sides. Move each magnet towards the north-pointing needle of the compass. If the needle moves slightly towards the magnet, this is a south pole. If the needle swings away from the magnet, this is a north pole. Mark the north side of each magnet with correction fluid.

5. Carefully place a ring magnet over each pencil, north pole down. Place a second set of magnets over the first set, south pole down. Notice how the second set of magnets floats over the first set, repelled by like poles. Continue with a third set of magnets, placed north pole down, and so on, until you have four stacks of floating magnets.
6. Top off your magnets with the thin Styrofoam board, placed so that the pencils fit through the holes and the board rests on the top set of magnets. You now have a platform supported by four magnetic "springs." Push down on the platform and test the cushioning effect the magnets produce.
7. Test the strength of your springs by placing some small objects on the platform, or slowly add coins to your platform. You will find that your magnetic springs can support quite a lot of weight before the magnets come together.

Electromagnetic springs like this will soon make up the shock absorbing systems of many cars. Linked to a computer in the engine, the spring for each wheel will adjust independently of the others.

Underground Bullet Train

Excited by the success of the tunnel linking Britain and France, scientists have bold plans for future tunnels. One futuristic idea uses an underground bullet train. This train would travel faster than the speed of sound — about 1,000 miles (1,609 km) per hour! A tunnel bored deep into the Earth would pass under oceans and continents, linking opposite sides of the world. The Earth's gravity would help a train achieve tremendous speed; then powerful superconducting electromagnets would keep it going and slow it down. Such a train, actually a giant electromagnetic coil, could use magnetic fields to power it.

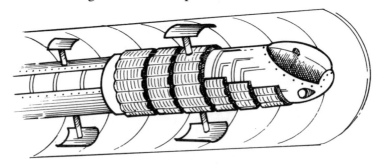

The Cyclotron

One of the greatest scientific achievements of the past 60 years has been the invention of the cyclotron, or "atom-smasher." This incredible machine makes it possible for scientists to glimpse into the nuclei of atoms in search of the single, smallest particle of matter. Recently, they've discovered such a particle: the quark.

A cyclotron consists of a thick-walled, giant tubelike ring, several miles long. Two beams of nuclei whirl in opposite directions inside the ring, accelerated and guided by powerful electromagnets. When the nuclei nearly reach the speed of light, the beams collide, and the nuclei smash apart into new, smaller particles.

Magnetic Recording

Today, everything from cassette tapes to credit cards contains information stored on a magnetic surface. Surprisingly, the invention of magnetic tape actually happened quite some time ago!

At the end of the nineteenth century, scientists discovered

that sound could be converted into a changing electro-magnetic field. Thomas Edison invented a machine that pulled a soft iron wire across an electromagnet. The particles in the wire changed positions, making a kind of magnetic fingerprint of the sounds. When the wire moved back against the electromagnet, the fingerprints changed back into electricity and turned back into sound. But Edison's invention produced such poor results that he abandoned the project.

A few years later, American and German inventors used a sticky strip of paper coated with iron particles. The sound quality was better, but it was difficult to make the iron particles small enough.

Today, the magnetic coating on recording tape consists of soft ferrites, ground to a fine powder. The finer the powder, the better the sound.

Inside Your Tape Recorder

An ordinary cassette tape recorder has two small, U-shaped electromagnets: one for recording and playing back and the other for erasing. When you speak or play music into the microphone of a tape recorder, the sound changes into electricity that travels into the recording magnet and creates a weak magnetic field. The two ends of the magnet, or *recording heads*, press against the tape as it rolls by. The magnetic field flowing out of these heads changes the positions of particles in a very precise way. When one physical process translates into another physical process, scientists call the process *analog* reproduction.

During playback, the tape rolls by the recording magnet again. But this time, the particles create an electrical current in the magnet, and the current changes back into sound.

The erasing magnet of a tape recorder is more powerful than the recording magnet. The *erasing heads* have to completely rearrange the particles of the recorded tape. When you record over a previously recorded tape, the tape first passes the erasing heads. They wipe it clean and prepare it to be magnetized again. But you'll get an even better recording if you first give your tape a "bath." Not really, of course, but if you hold your tape against a strong electromagnet, you'll get the best erasing results and less "hiss" when you record over the tape again. Recording technicians often use such large magnets to erase many tapes at once.

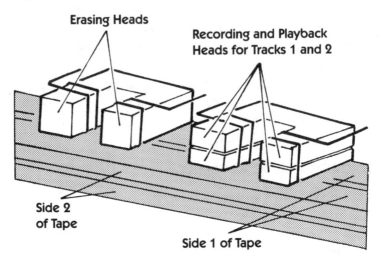

Erasing Heads

Recording and Playback
Heads for Tracks 1 and 2

Side 2
of Tape

Side 1 of Tape

Floppy and Hard Disks

Recording on magnetic computer disks resembles recording on magnetic tapes. Ferrites coat both floppy and hard disks. One advantage of disks over tape is that information is easy to find. The writing/reading magnet of a computer (equal to the recording/playback magnet of a tape recorder) moves quickly to the right section of the disk. When you use a tape recorder, you have to rewind the tape to get there.

Unlike recording on tape, or analog reproduction, writing to disk is a *digital* process. Computers operate on the binary system of 1s and 0s, using only these numbers. So a magnetic disk contains not sounds, but a simple "on" and "off" arrangement of particles. Long chains of these represent long chains of 1s and 0s. This creates a binary set of instructions that tells the computer what to do.

You can easily show the effect a strong magnetic field has on recording tape by building an electromagnetic tape eraser. This handy instrument will allow you to erase cassette tapes quickly and thoroughly. Warning: A powerful erasing machine should never operate near tapes, computers, or computer disks.

ELECTROMAGNETIC TAPE ERASER

You Will Need
Steel U-bolt with plate
and nuts ¼ × 2½
inches (.6 × 6 cm)
10 feet (3m) of insulated
copper wire

Scissors
Electrical tape
6-volt battery
Compass

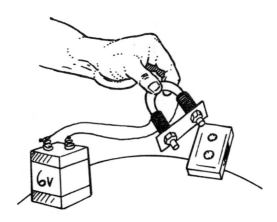

1. Remove the nuts and plate from the U-bolt. On the floor, stretch out the 10 feet (3m) of copper wire and place the U-bolt in the middle.

2. Coil four layers of wire around each leg of the U-bolt, leaving ½ inch (1.25cm) space at the ends for the nuts. Make sure you wrap both coils in the same direction, following the diagram.

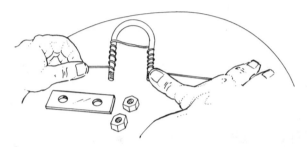

3. Cover the coils with electrical tape to keep the wire from unwinding.

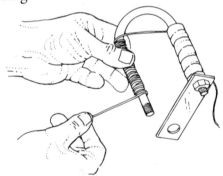

4. With the scissors, carefully cut ½-inch (1.2 cm) of plastic coating from the ends of the wire. Attach those ends to the battery terminals.

5. Put the plate back on the ends of the U-bolt, against the taped coils of wire. Screw the nuts at the ends of the bolt over the plate.

6. Use a compass to test the poles of your electromagnet. One should be a north pole and the other a south pole. If you have two of the same poles, you wound the second

coil in the wrong direction and need to rewind it.

7. Test your electromagnet by holding a few iron objects near to it. The force of the attraction will surprise you.

Tape Erasing

It takes only a few seconds for a magnet of this strength to completely erase a tape cassette. Hold the cassette against the poles and notice how strongly it attracts. Slide the tape forward, backwards, and sideways for a few seconds. You don't have to turn the tape over to erase the other side.

Superconductors

Earlier, we mentioned a space project called Jacob's Ladder. To build such a futuristic machine, scientists need some special ingredients — among them, superpowerful, lightweight electromagnets. Recently, they've created materials that make such magnets possible. Called *superconductors*, these materials consist of mixtures of rare earth metals cooled with liquid helium or liquid nitrogen. At such low temperatures, all electrical resistance vanishes, and the metals become pure conductors of electromagnetic energy.

Because they must be kept so cold, there aren't a lot of ways to use superconductors. But a few metals can turn into superconductors at higher temperatures. One of these, yttrium, shows great promise as the perfect superconductor.

Magnets in Medicine

Scientists have long dreamt of "seeing through walls." At the end of the nineteenth century, scientists thought the dream might come true. X rays penetrated human tissue but not bone. For the first time, doctors could examine broken bones through flesh. They could also look for other problems without having to operate on a patient. X rays can damage human tissue though, and soon scientists began to explore other ideas.

Thanks to magnets, scientists have developed a machine that peers deep inside the human body without harming it. This machine can find diseased areas long before they would show up on an ordinary X ray. Scientists named the machine the MRI Scanner. MRI stands for *magnetic resonance imaging*.

Made from superconductors, an MRI electromagnet looks like a giant doughnut. The person receiving the MRI scan lies in the hole of the doughnut while the doughnut slowly moves back and forth, collecting information and creating pictures. These pictures appear on a computer screen for the doctor to examine.

MRI electromagnets are among the most powerful magnets ever built. In fact, the magnetic fields are so powerful that the magnets must operate within protected chambers. Scientists realized this after hospital workers reported pens, scissors, surgical instruments, even fire extinguishers tumbling down hallways when a magnet was working!

How It Works

When we talked about paramagnetism and diamagnetism (pages 15–17), we learned that a strong magnetic field can move the atoms in a material, even though the material itself may not show any attraction to the magnet. In fact, diamagnetic materials, such as human tissue, actually turn their atoms away from the magnetic field.

When scientists switch on an MRI electromagnet, the atoms in human tissue "turn their backs" to it. A radio wave, beamed at the tissue from a different angle, excites only hydrogen atoms, causing them to turn towards the magnet, just a little. When the radio wave stops, the hydrogen atoms turn away again.

The MRI computer measures the time it takes the hydrogen atoms to turn away the second time. Scientists know that hydrogen atoms in diseased tissue take longer to return to their original positions than hydrogen atoms in healthy tissue. The computer can put this time difference into a picture that shows the location of diseased tissue. All this, and the patient doesn't feel a thing!

Magnetism and Nuclear Energy

The atomic age began when scientists learned to control the release of nuclear energy. The splitting and fusing of atoms promised huge amounts of energy. And since atoms are everywhere, our supply of "fuel" should never run out. But atomic reactions also need great amounts of energy to start them and keep them going. This energy, in the form of heat, has to be at a dangerously high level. No solid container can hold such heat. No material on Earth can survive the temperature (close to the Sun's) of an atomic reaction.

The answer? Magnets, of course! Scientists used them to create a special magnetic field called a *magnetic bottle*. The field, actually shaped like a bottle, has a charge that repels the extremely hot particles and contains them during the atomic reaction.

Magnets in Archaeological Dating

By studying the rings of ancient trees, scientists can learn a great deal about weather patterns thousands of years ago. In a similar way, they can tell where the North Pole was in the distant past. They do this by looking at ancient geological structures, called clay banks, that contain iron particles.

Like tiny compass needles frozen in time, these particles aligned themselves to the Earth's magnetic field long ago. Once the clay set, the particles stayed in position. When scientists study the clay, they see the particles all pointing to an ancient north pole. By comparing the position of the particles with the position of a modern compass needle, they can figure out the location of that ancient pole.

The particles point in different directions, depending on the age of the clay. Over a span of several thousand years, scientists can estimate where the North Pole was and how it moved.

Ancient pieces of pottery also contain iron particles. Firing the pottery in a kiln set the particles. Each time an

archaeologist finds a piece of pottery, he carefully notes its position in the ground in relation to the North Pole. He must do this accurately before he removes the pottery from its site. Then a small piece of clay is broken off for study.

By looking at the particles, while taking into account the original position of the pottery, a good archaeologist can figure out where the North Pole was when the clay hardened. Comparing this with other data, and with the position of the North Pole today, he can estimate just how long ago this particular potter practiced his trade. This fancy trick has a fancy name: *thermoremanent magnetic dating*.

Outsmarting Ocean Bombs

During World War II, enemy mines often damaged British and American warships. The usual type of mine floated on the surface of the water and was hard to see, especially at night. But in 1940, the Nazis designed an even deadlier mine. They began dropping these mines into the Thames River where they sank to the bottom. In addition to being invisible, the bombs knew exactly when to explode.

When scientists finally brought one up and studied it, they discovered that it had an inclinometer, or "dip compass," attached to it. The inclinometer, aligned to the Earth's magnetic field, was the key. When a large ship passed overhead, the magnetized iron of its hull would change the position of the inclinometer needle, triggering the explosive.

Scientists had a tough job ahead. They had to figure out how to demagnetize a ship's iron hull so that it could pass over a mine without moving the needle. Fifty years ago the technique was called *degaussing*, from an old-fashioned unit of magnetic-field measurement called the *gauss*. Today, scientists call it *magnetic neutralizing*.

The trick consists of demagnetizing the iron parts during a ship's construction, then wrapping a coil around the completed ship's hull. Generators pass an electrical current through the coil in carefully measured amounts to make the ship magnetically invisible. A computer calculates the voltage according to how long the ship has travelled or been docked in a particular direction relative to the Earth's poles.

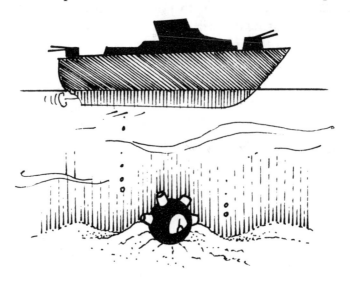

Liquid Crystals

Imagine a sparkling clear plate-glass window that can dim and turn completely black with the push of a button. Actually, you've already seen such a thing on a small scale — the so-called liquid crystal display (LCD) of a digital wristwatch.

Crystals, along with some liquids and gases, can change in odd ways when exposed to magnetic fields. The way each substance changes has to do with the shape and size of its molecules. For example, the crystal potassium dihydrogen phosphate consists of large, irregular molecules in a random arrangement. When held in an electromagnetic field, these molecules all turn in the same direction. This changes the transparency of the crystal, in effect shutting out the light like closing a shutter.

This change is even greater in the liquid nitrobenzene. Like a crystal, it has large, irregular molecules. Scientists call substances like nitrobenzene *liquid crystals*. When held in an electromagnetic field, nitrobenzene molecules turn in the same direction and shut out the light.

Most digital wristwatches and portable computer-game screens use small chambers of nitrobenzene connected to a weak electric current. Maybe in the future, scientists will construct large sheets of crystalline material that act the same way.

Looking to the Future

With so many amazing inventions, it's hard to imagine the science of magnetism going much further. But new discoveries will certainly change the way most people live and think about the world. Scientists hope to learn much more about one of our planet's greatest resources — its magnetic field. What created this huge, powerful force of nature? Can it be changed to repair the atmosphere or improve weather patterns? Will scientists have the power, someday, to close the polar holes in the ozone layer? Or create unlimited electrical energy? Or hurl spacecrafts far into space without fuel?

Plasma magnetics is a fascinating new area of study. Scientists may someday learn how to magnetize water so that it attracts substances, both beneficial and harmful. During an electrical storm, lightning charges the water droplets so that more nitrogen sticks to them. A thunderstorm's cloudburst contains nitrogen-rich nutrients, good for plants. Could magnetized rain attract pollutants and truly cleanse the air with each new downpour? Could magnetized rivers change direction and flow uphill? Someday, we'll have the answers for these and other questions.

Glossary

Alloy. A new substance made from a combination of two or more metals, or a combination of metals with nonmetals. Alloys are designed to improve the strength, flexibility, or magnetic response of the original materials.

Alternating current. Electrical current that reverses its direction of flow many times per second. A crude variety of AC current was first produced by Michael Faraday's electric dynamo.

Analog reproduction. A method of translating information from one physical quantity into another. In magnetic tape recording, for example, sound vibrations move the diaphragm of a microphone, which then translates the vibrations into a changing electrical current. The current flows through coils on the recording head and creates a magnetic field. The field changes the positions of ferrite particles on the tape and leaves a magnetic fingerprint of the original sound. *Compare with Digital reproduction.*

Armature. The moving part of an electric motor containing the electromagnetic coil and contact brushes.

Atom smasher. Also called a cyclotron. A large, tubular chamber that uses electromagnets to accelerate two beams of atomic nuclei in opposite directions. The beams are then made to collide, breaking the nuclei into smaller particles.

Atomic particles. The electrically charged parts of an atom. These include the electrons, the nucleus, and particles within the nucleus.

Attraction. The "pull" of magnet towards magnet at opposite poles, or the pull of a magnet towards ferromagnetic metals. On an atomic scale, the shifting of the magnetic atoms in a substance towards a magnet.

Bismuth. A diamagnetic metal with a net magnetic moment of close to zero.

Cardinal points. The North, South, East, and West direction indicators of a compass, placed 90 degrees apart.

Charges in motion. The movement of electrically charged particles in the atom, such as electrons revolving about the nucleus, electrons spinning about their axis, or nuclear particles spinning within the nucleus. Each spinning particle contributes a magnetic moment to the larger atom, but the magnetic moment of a particle may be cancelled out by a particle spinning in the opposite direction.

Commutator. The part of an electric motor made from two strips of conducting metal that touch the contact brushes of the armature. The strips are separated just enough so that contact with the brushes is broken twice during each revolution of the armature. This allows the poles of the armature coil to reverse.

Compass card. In a radial compass, the circular card beneath the compass needle that indicates cardinal points and degrees between cardinal points.

Curie temperature. The high temperature at which a ferromagnetic metal loses its potential to become a magnet or to retain magnetism. Different metals have different Curie temperatures.

Degaussing. An out-of-date term for demagnetizing iron based on an obsolete unit of magnetic measurement, the gauss. *See Magnetic neutralizing.*

Diamagnetism. The most subtle form of magnetic response and the natural magnetic quality of all matter. For reasons still unknown, the magnetically neutral atoms of diamagnetic materials shift slightly away from a strong outside magnet.

Digital reproduction. A method of translating information into an "on" and "off" arrangement of particles, or switches, on a magnetic computer disk. The switches represent the 1s and 0s of a binary code, and long chains of these digits represent the original information mathematically. *Compare with Analog reproduction.*

Dip compass. Also called an inclinometer. A vertical compass that helps navigators calculate distance to a magnetic pole. The compass needle dips sharply near a pole and less sharply near the equator. The degree of dip is indicated on a circular scale that surrounds the needle. *Compare with Radial compass.*

Dipolarity. A basic physical property of magnets wherein the poles of the magnetic field always occur in opposite pairs and can never exist independently of each other.

Domains. The natural organization of magnetized atoms in ferromagnetic, but unmagnetized, metals. The atoms come together in millions of cluster formations, with all the atoms of a single cluster pointing in the same general direction. The clusters themselves do not align, however, and so the metal shows no obvious magnetic qualities.

Electromagnet/electromagnetism. Magnetism produced when an electrical current flows through a coil of conducting material, such as copper wire. The coil of wire then becomes an electromagnet, with north and south poles, but its magnetism lasts only as long as the current flows through it. *Compare with Permanent magnets.*

Electron. A negatively charged particle that moves about the nucleus of an atom.

Element. Any of more than 100 fundamental substances, including the pure metals, that consist of atoms of only one kind. The elements, alone or in combination, make up all matter in the universe.

Erase/record heads. The small, U-shaped electromagnets in a tape recorder against which the magnetic tape moves. The erasing head, with its steady magnetic field, is the stronger magnet of the two. It erases any magnetic patterns before the tape moves on to the recording head. The recording head has a changing magnetic field that creates patterns on the ferrite coating of the tape. *See Write/read magnets.*

Faraday, Michael. The Nineteenth Century British scientist who discovered the principle of induction, or how electrical current is produced in a conducting material when a magnet moves near it. This led to Faraday's design for the first electrical generator: the "magnetic dynamo." *See Induction.*

Ferrimagnetism. The magnetic quality of ferrites, a class of crystalline metallic substances that includes the magnetite of lodestones. Ferrimagnetic materials consist of strong and weak magnetic atoms. When exposed to an outside magnet, the strong atoms turn towards the magnet while the weaker atoms shift away. This odd effect is due to the unusual crystalline structure of the ferrite molecules.

Ferrite. A class of crystalline metallic substances that includes the magnetite of lodestones. Powdered ferrites coat magnetic recording tape and computer disks.

Ferromagnetism. The magnetic quality of iron, nickel, and cobalt — all metals composed of strongly magnetic atoms and all easily turned into magnets.

Field magnets. On an electrical motor, the stationary magnets that lie on opposite sides of the revolving armature. The field magnets provide a permanent magnetic field that interacts with the electromagnetic field of the armature coil.

Galvanometer. An instrument that detects, by the movement of its needle, the presence of an electrical current.

Geocentric. A motion that follows exactly the Earth's rotation. A geocentric satellite does not revolve around the Earth, but with it.

Geographic north/south pole. The fixed extremities of the Earth's axis, as indicated on maps, and the origin of the global coordinates longitude and latitude. *Compare with Magnetic north/south pole.*

Gimbal ring. A pivoting ring or pair of rings that surrounds a radial compass and keeps it level in turbulence.

High reluctance. The physical property of materials that do not easily transmit magnetic lines of force, such as glass, wood, ceramics, and non-magnetic metals.

Inclinometer. *See Dip compass.*

Induction. The process of creating electricity by moving a magnet against a conducting material, such as copper. The induction principle was discovered by the Nineteenth Century British scientist Michael Faraday and is the basis of all electrical generators.

Lodestone. A stone made of magnetite, a naturally magnetic (but not ferromagnetic) material in a metallic class of substances called ferrites. Although the peculiar ferrimagnetic properties of the ferrites make them weaker magnets, lodestones were probably used for the first compasses.

Low reluctance. The physical property of materials that easily transmit magnetic lines of force, such as iron, nickel, cobalt, and alloys of those metals. Low reluctance materials are used as magnetic insulators in electrical wires. Electromagnetic lines of force are drawn into the material and do not leak out into the surrounding air.

Magnetic bottle. An electromagnetic field that is designed to surround and contain high-temperature atomic reactions.

Magnetic cells. Cells containing magnetite in the bodies of animals. Scientists believe that these cells help some animals, such as dolphins and whales, navigate by sensing the Earth's magnetic field.

Magnetic dynamo. The first electric generator, designed by the Nineteenth-Century English scientist Michael Faraday. The dynamo produced a crude alternating current by moving a magnet back and forth within a copper coil.

Magnetic field. Magnetic lines of force that flow around permanent magnets, electromagnets, electrical conductors, and the Earth. The lines of force in a magnetic field concentrate at opposite ends, or poles, of the magnet and can never be separated.

Magnetic moment. The spin of an atomic particle around its axis, which is either reinforced by the spin of a second atomic particle, or cancelled by it. Many atomic particles, spinning in the same direction, create a magnetic field around the atom, and, in effect, turn the atom into a magnet. *See Charges in motion.*

Magnetic neutralizing. The technique of using carefully controlled electrical current to demagnetize the iron hulls of ships in order to make them less susceptible to magnetically triggered explosive devices. *See Degaussing.*

Magnetic north/south pole. Two drifting regions, roughly opposite each other, where the Earth's magnetic field concentrates. Magnetic poles differ in location from geographic poles, which are fixed regions at the extremities of the Earth's axis. A compass always points to a magnetic pole, not a geographical one, and this degree of error must be taken into account when navigating. *See Magnetic variation.*

Magnetic resonance imaging (MRI). A technique for seeing inside the human body by placing it in a strong magnetic field. Excited by the field, hydrogen atoms in the body shift, then shift again as a second beam of radio waves bombards them. When the radio beam stops, the atoms snap back to their first position — except for the atoms in diseased tissue, which return to their positions slowly. A computer translates this time difference into an image, highlighting the diseased tissue.

Magnetic suspension. A magnetic cushion produced by aligning a series of magnets with like poles facing each other. Scientists can manipulate electromagnets in the same way, creating a force of repulsion strong enough to lift thousands of pounds — a principle now used to levitate high-speed trains.

Magnetic variation. The distance, measured in degrees, between a geographic pole and a magnetic pole. A navigator must take into account this margin of error when using a compass to determine direction accurately.

Magnetite. A naturally magnetic (but not ferromagnetic) crystalline material in a metallic class of substances called ferrites. Magnetite is created by iron-eating bacteria that die and leave magnetite deposits behind. It is also found in the cells of many animals, leading scientists to suspect that it aids in animal navigation. Although this material is magnetically weaker than any of the ferromagnetic metals, magnetite, in the form of lodestones, was probably used for the first compasses. *See Lodestone.*

Magnetometer. A sensitive measuring device designed to detect magnetic response, particularly the weak response of paramagnetic metals.

Micrometeorites. Meteorites too small and too light to burn up as they enter the Earth's atmosphere. Most float in the air and fall to the ground only when they stick to water droplets or dust particles. Micrometeorites can be either magnetic or non-magnetic and fall into four categories: siderites, stony meteorites, siderolites, and asideres.

Net magnetic moment. The relative magnetic strength of an atom, determined by the combined spins of the atom's charged particles. When particles spin in the same direction, they contribute to the atom's magnetic strength; when particles spin in opposite directions, they detract or cancel out the atom's magnetism. *See Magnetic moment.*

Nucleus. The positively charged central part of an atom around which the electrons revolve. The nucleus is not a single particle, but made of independently spinning particles.

Oersted, Hans. The Nineteenth Century Danish doctor who discovered, quite by accident, the connection between magnetism and electricity. In a demonstration to prove that the two forces were not related, he ran electrical current through a wire, which caused a compass needle to jump away from its north-seeking direction. This suggested that the electrical flow in the wire had produced a magnetic field similar to that of the Earth. *See Galvanometer.*

Paramagnetism. The slight magnetic response of metals, such as copper, aluminum, and gold, that are composed of weakly magnetized atoms. This response is only detected by a sensitive instrument called a magnetometer. Paramagnetic metals behave more like ferromagnetic metals when cooled. The cooling slows the natural random movements of the atoms and allows the atoms to align.

Permanent magnets. Magnets made of ferromagnetic metals or their alloys, shaped variously, that react with other magnets or with metals. A permanent magnet produces a steady flow of force around itself, called the magnetic field, that comes together at opposite sides of the magnet, or poles. Permanent magnets attract each other at opposite poles, and repel at like poles. *Compare with Electromagnet/electromagnetism.*

Pure metals. Metals that are not combined with other metals or non-metals and belong to a group of fundamental substances known as the elements. *See Element.*

Radial compass. Ordinary navigator's compass that lies flat against a horizontal surface and indicates magnetic north by way of a pivoting, magnetized needle. The circular compass card behind the needle is divided into degrees between cardinal points. *Compare* *with Dip compass.*

Rare earth metals. A class of mostly paramagnetic substances, occurring naturally in soil and in rock deposits, that show strong ferromagnetic-like qualities when cooled to extremely low temperatures. When used in electromagnets, the cooling of these metals enhances the flow of electrical current through them, creating a condition called superconductivity. This enhanced flow leads to an extremely powerful electromagnetic field. *See Superconductor.*

Repulsion. The "push" of magnet away from magnet at like poles. On an atomic scale, the shifting of the magnetic atoms in a substance away from a magnet.

Superconductor. A rare earth metal cooled to an extremely low temperature by liquid nitrogen or liquid helium. This cooling allows for an enhanced flow of electrical current through the metal, which creates an extremely powerful electromagnet. *See Rare earth metals.*

Thermoremanent magnetic dating. A technique for dating ancient clay artifacts by examining the orientation of iron particles in the clay with respect to the present-day location of the north and south poles.

Write/read magnets. The magnets attached to the moving arm mechanism inside a computer and similar in function to the erase/record heads of a tape recorder. In this case, however, the magnets float over the floppy or hard disk and can drop down to any section of the disk to write or read information. The information is coded on the disk's ferrite surface in binary form. *See Digital reproduction.*

Experiment Abstracts

Electromagnetic Tape Eraser (pp. 107–109). Demonstrates the usefulness, and dangers, of a strong electromagnetic field applied to magnetic recording tape.

Ferromagnetic Scavenger Hunt (pp. 7–9). A hunt for everyday items that helps you become aware of magnetic materials in your environment.

Floating Platform (pp. 101–103). Demonstrates a practical use of magnetic repulsion in shock-absorbing devices.

Flying Paper Clip (pp. 76–77). A dramatic demonstration of how invisible magnetic lines of force travel through the air.

Flow Chart for Magnetism (pp. 25–26). A chart that helps you sort through everyday items in order to discover which ones are ferromagnetic, and why.

Just Passing Through (pp. 40–41). Shows how magnetic lines of force are affected when magnets are covered with various materials.

Keep Apart, Keep Together (pp. 45–46). Ball bearings and bar magnets demonstrate a surprising change in the usual behavior of a magnetic field.

Levitating Ladies (pp. 74–76). Demonstrates the peculiar phenomenon of magnetic repulsion between like poles of bar magnets.

Lifting a Chair (pp. 23–24). Shows why the design of horseshoe and U-shaped magnets makes for better lifting power.

Magic Thumbtack (pp. 46–47). Shows how magnetic lines of force can jump from a large object into a smaller one, becoming more concentrated.

Magnet Making (pp. 12–14). Learn to understand the principles behind permanent magnets and electromagnets by making one of each.

Magnetic Dynamo (pp. 62–64). The principle of induction shown by moving a bar magnet through a coil of wire in order to create electrical current in the wire.

Magnetic Pictures (pp. 29–30). Iron filings help you observe the invisible magnetic fields surrounding variously shaped magnets.

Magnetism — Now You See It . . . (pp. 42–43). Demonstrates magnetic insulation, or how you can direct magnetic lines of force away from something and into something else.

Micrometeorite Collecting (pp. 98–100). Examines the strange world of magnetic and non-magnetic micrometeors by collecting rainwater, evaporating it, and examining the particles with a microscope or magnifying glass.

Push and Pull (pp. 32–33). Traces magnetic lines of force through the air with the help of two strong bar magnets and iron filings.

Recreating Earth's Magnetic Field (pp. 27–28). A dramatic demonstration that shows, with the help a bar magnet and iron filings, the shape of the Earth's magnetic field.

Rock Hunting (pp. 19–20). An outdoor search for natural magnets, or lodestones, and how to recognize them using a compass.

Rust and Sand (pp. 49–50). Shows how magnetic filtering works by using a horseshoe magnet to separate ferromagnetic rust particles from sand.

Soil Separator (pp. 57–59). Learn how to separate interesting magnetic particles from ordinary soil with the help of a U-shaped magnet, garden spade, and two water-filled jars.

Sorcerer's Apprentice Test (pp. 30–31). An experiment that breaks a large magnet into smaller ones to show that every piece has a north and south pole and is a miniature magnet.

Spool and Thread Motor (pp. 65–72). Build a working model that puts many important magnetic principles to practical use.

String of Beads (pp. 44–45). Shows how to extend a magnetic field downwards by adding steel ball bearings to the end of a bar magnet.

Tricks with Rulers (pp. 47–48). With steel rulers and bar magnets, learn how magnetic fields adapt their behavior to peculiar conditions.

Water Compass (pp. 52–55). Build a working model of a radial compass and learn more about compass design, construction, and operation.

World in a Tin Can (pp. 50–51). Demonstrates how ferromagnetic metals are naturally magnetized by the Earth's magnetic field.

Index